HR Business Partners

HR Business Partners

IAN HUNTER, JANE SAUNDERS,
ALLAN BOROUGHS AND
SIMON CONSTANCE

 Routledge
Taylor & Francis Group

LONDON AND NEW YORK

First published in paperback 2024

First published 2006 by Gower Publishing

Published 2016 by Routledge
4 Park Square, Milton Park, Abingdon, Oxon OX14 4RN

and by Routledge
605 Third Avenue, New York, NY 10158

Routledge is an imprint of the Taylor & Francis Group, an informa business

British Library Cataloguing in Publication Data
HR business partners: emerging service delivery models
   for the HR function
   1. Personnel management
   I. Hunter, Ian
   658.3

Library of Congress Control Number: 2005928467

ISBN 13: 978-0-566-08625-0 (hbk)
ISBN 13: 978-1-03-283763-5 (pbk)
ISBN 13: 978-1-315-58724-0 (ebk)

DOI: 10.4324/9781315587240

Typeset by IML Typographers, Birkenhead, Merseyside.

Contents

List of Figures

List of Tables

Acknowledgements

The authors would like to warmly thank the following for their help and advice during the writing of this book.

Jonathan Norman, Nikki Dines and Helen Parry from Gower for their help in structuring and editing the manuscript.

Peter Upton from Orion Partners for his thoughts on the perspective of the line manager.

For agreeing to be interviewed during the research for this book we would particularly like to thank: James Bennett (Oracle); Mike Clements; Avery Duff; Dan Flint; Hugh Hood; Malcolm Howard; Rod James; Vance Kearney; Jenni Lehman (PeopleSoft); Dominic Mahony; Russell Martin; Bob Mason; John Maxted; Cathy McNullty; Howard Nelson; Thomas Otter (SAP); Lucy Poloniecka; Angela Spelman; Joel Summer (Oracle); Joanne Tucker; Liz Wilson (PeopleSoft) and Brian Wishart. Our thanks should also be recorded to the many others who agreed to participate in the research but requested the protective blanket of anonymity.

CHAPTER 1

The Evolution of HR

This book addresses the key challenge facing the HR profession in the early twenty-first century. Arguably the most important issue for HR, rather than the oft-quoted ones of changing demographics and employee commitment, is how the HR function should organize itself to tackle the questions that the modern world and business environment asks of it. If the HR function gets it right the opportunities are as endless as the creativity of the HR professionals in the function. Should it fail to rise to the challenge, many commentators believe that the writing is on the wall for HR's status as an activity that deserves a place at the boardroom table.[1]

The space in which HR has traditionally operated has changed. This book explores a model that will keep HR at the top table and assist its leaders to deliver opportunities for improving organizational and people performance – the key sources of competitive advantage and success for organizations in the future.

The business, working and commercial environment in both the private and public sectors has altered dramatically in the last 20 years. Firms experienced the dot.com bubble, where the certainties of what made a successful business model seemed to fundamentally shift, and then did not. Technology and the pace of working life have moved up several gears, placing demands on employees, in terms of expanding the scope of their roles and compressing the time they have to make decisions. Knowledge is frequently referred to as the last remaining source of competitive advantage.[2] In the broader business environment, globalization is a reality that has an impact on every organization, both public and private.[3] Even if it does not affect us in terms of direct competition from other new international entrants to the marketplace, globalization forces upon us a culture of benchmarking with the 'best in the world'. Executives from the US and Europe are taking leading roles in running British companies and, more significantly, public sector organizations. Operating performance comparisons are no longer set against local competitors or providers, but against countries that have seemingly unassailable competitive advantages in areas like labour costs and technology. The bar for assessing individual and organizational performance is continually rising.

---

1 'HR Survey. Where we are, where we're heading'. Chartered Institute of Personnel and Development (CIPD), October 2003. Ulrich, D. (1997) *Human Resource Champions: The Next Agenda for Adding Value and Delivering Results*, Harvard Business School Press.

2 Evans, P. and Wurster, T.S. (2000) *Blown to Bits: How the New Economics of Information Transform Strategy*, Harvard Business School Press.

3 Scase, R. (2002) *Living in the Corporate Zoo: Life and Work in 2010*, Capstone Publishing Ltd.

What has not changed though is the fact that people are still the engine which drives an organization to grow, excel and ultimately succeed or fail. Even the great (certainly infamous) managers of modern times (for example, Gerstner at IBM and Welch at GE) cite the performance of their people as being the key to success.[4]

> Admiral Insurance is a company that has sought to exploit the aftermath of the dot.com boom and tackle the entrenched market leaders, and it has been highly successful. Prior to a flotation that saw a majority of employees acquire in significant holdings in the company, in an interview with *The Sunday Times*, Henry Englehardt, CEO of Admiral Insurance, talked about what had made the company so successful. He simply said: 'The trick in this business is good people ... the numbers don't do it for themselves'.[5]

For HR professionals Englehardt's statement may seem a truism. HR professionals invest their careers in bringing that quote to life and yet, amongst all the change, there is a feeling that HR still has not been able to deliver what is self-evident. Commentators on the activities of HR functions have been building a consensus that HR is 'heading towards a precipice', and that it is time 'to sort the men out from the boys in the HR function'.[6] Even senior practitioners comment that HR still has to raise its game.

> 'We have really started to link people processes to business results ... It's only the capability, or lack of it, of the HR Business Partners that means we aren't maximising the linkages' – HR strategy director, global investment bank
>
> 'HR is apologetic and insecure' – HRD, major insurance company
>
> 'The first way to an easy life is to be crap. If you're skills aren't relevant, then neither are you and the business will get on without you' – HRD, global software organization[7]

Changes in the competitive and working environment have required the HR function to rethink how it organizes itself to meet these new challenges. This book seeks to explore the impact of these challenges on the HR function and to outline a model that allows the function to place itself at the centre of maximizing its organization's

---

4 Gerstner, L.V. (2002) *Who Says Elephants Can't Dance?*, HarperCollins Publishers. Welch, J. (2001) *Jack: What I've Learned from Leading a Great Company and Great People*, Headline.

5 Davidson, A. (2004) 'Buy Admiral shares or you will need insurance', *The Sunday Times*, 12 September.

6 'HR Survey. Where we are, where we're heading.' Chartered Institute of Personnel and Development, October 2003.

7 These quotes are from research on the challenges for HR conducted by Orion Partners (2004) amongst HR Directors (HRDs) at a range of major organizations.

effectiveness as it delivers for its stakeholders. At the heart of this new challenge is the concept of HR Business Partnering (HR BP).

In examining the HR Business Partnering model, we shall review the theory behind the role and how that sits with the evolution of thinking around how HR organizes itself. The role of HR strategy will be examined with a strong focus on practice. We shall also address the issue of transformation: how to move a function to the model outlined. Much has been written and spoken about the rise of HR shared services, HR outsourcing and HR Information Systems (HRIS) and we shall assess the interaction of the HR BP and these three aspects of HR operations. Finally, the skills required, development paths available and approaches to career management are reviewed in order to provide a pragmatic approach to implementation.

WHO WE ARE

Orion Partners LLP are the leading European adviser on HR transformation. We specialize in defining and implementing HR BP programmes, HR outsourcing arrangements, HR Shared Services and supporting the assessment and selection of HR Information Systems platforms.

Fully independent, we act as an impartial guide through the myriad of options open to clients. We offer an objective assessment of suppliers and solutions related to a firm's individual needs. We work alongside client staff to implement a solution capable of delivering the intended results. And, significantly, we work directly with the HR team to help develop the skills and confidence necessary to operate in a new environment.

Out specialist team offers a collective source of expertise unrivalled in the market. With blue-chip HR practitioner and international consulting firm backgrounds, we have direct experience of formulating and managing some of the most high-profile and complex outsourcing and Shared Service deals currently in operation.

WHERE IS HR TODAY?

Current thinking and practice about its role, purpose and structure reveals that HR has been on a transformational journey over the last 30 years. Although there is no one recognized map to this challenging trip, a number of common milestones can be identified that mark significant changes in the perception and focus of the function, both in the UK and in all other industrialized nations.

HUMAN RESOURCE MANAGEMENT – THE BEGINNING OF CHANGE

Prior to the early 1960s, Personnel was seen as an administrative function (for example, payroll or time-keeping administration). With the industrial unrest and rapidly changing labour legislation of the 1960s and 1970s the role of the Personnel function as a 'policeman' of labour relations in the workplace rose to prominence.[8] It was not until the early 1980s that a new approach to Personnel started to develop. This period saw the rise of Human Resource Management (HRM).

Human Resource Management as a distinct managerial approach drew on two themes in the 1980s that still resonate in HR's goals and aspirations today. The first of these was an attempt to link HR activities to business outcomes. The second is the Harvard model which sought to acknowledge the complex interactions between all the parties involved in people management. The common thread between the two themes is the desire to refocus the activities of the Personnel function onto supporting the delivery of business strategy. By doing this, HR can fulfil better the aspirations of organizational stakeholders and exploit the potential of putting people management at the heart of business success.

Though initially unsophisticated in its approach, Charles Fombrum, Noel Tichy and Mary Anne DeVanna attempt to link the key policy and activity areas of HR to delivering the business strategy.[9] They sought to map out the links that HR could use to channel behaviour in a way that was supportive of the organization's strategy. In this model employee performance is directed by the appropriate Personnel interventions, from the start of the employee's relationship with the company at their selection, through to the influences on their pay packet.

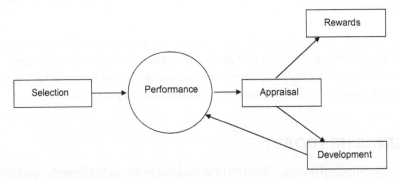

Figure 1.1   Fombrum, Tichy and DeVanna's model of the HR cycle[10]

---

8   Hendry, C. (1995) *A Strategic Approach to Employment*, Butterworth Heinemann. Ulrich, D. and Beatty, D. (2001) 'From Partners to Players: Extending the HR Playing Field'. *Human Resource Management*, Winter.

9   Fombrum, C., Tichy, N. and DeVanna, M.A. (1981) *Human Resource Management: A Strategic Perspective*, Wenter.

10 Hendry, C. (1995) *A Strategic Approach to Employment*, Butterworth Heinemann.

Whilst this model contained little analysis of how the mechanics of each activity affected employee performance, it was an important signpost to the direction of future thinking and a dramatic shift from the prevailing reactive nature of the profession where Personnel managers typically responded to requests made by their customers rather than actively seeking to anticipate and shape requirements.

This alignment of employee workplace action and behaviour placed HR processes at the heart of the search for competitive advantage.

The second model that emerged in the 1980s to assist the change in HR's aspiration shifted its focus to the employee as a 'human resource'. Here staff were seen as having a potential to develop and express individual needs.[11] This approach was developed at Harvard University as an element of the MBA programme by academics such as Professor Michael Beer. It clearly opens avenues for a more sophisticated analysis of how the Personnel function might have an impact on the business's strategy. Once it is acknowledged that employee interaction occurs on an individual level, involving 'actors' such as senior managers, line managers, Personnel staff and colleagues, a more robust model of directing employee performance can be developed as the influences on these parties can be more accurately assessed and implemented.

This Harvard School of HRM moved the focus away from HR processes and systems and into a model that sought to manage through developing high commitment amongst employees. Through this form of engagement, each individual could be harnessed to drive business performance as the commitment of the employee was aligned with the goals and strategy of the organization for which they worked. Whilst still crude, in that it assumes that employees across all sectors and level wish to be 'committed', it once again proposed that people management can directly drive business performance.

As a result of the development of these models and research into their practical application, particularly in the United States, the means for HR to effect an organiz-ation's performance opened up. Executive expectations about what HR could provide were widened. As HR professionals applied these theories in practice, they found themselves moving away from a skill set and career path that had been rooted in manpower planning, reactive industrial relations management and administration. As practitioners moved to align HR activity with the organization's objectives, HR professionals needed to be able evaluate different solutions and identify the drivers and stakeholders which had the best impact. The need to prove quantifiably that HR added value to the bottom and top line of the balance sheet was a new challenge. Traditionally the career path of most HR professionals and the job descriptions they had been fulfilling had not provided them with the toolkit to do that.

---

11   Hendry, C. (1995) *A Strategic Approach to Employment*, Butterworth Heinemann.

HOW STRATEGIC ARE HR PROFESSIONALS TODAY? THE CASE FOR CHANGE

The changing nature of the HR role in its approach to supporting the business has been identified, but what about the activities of those who lead the profession? If HR is looking to make the case for the role of people management in improving business performance, the position and role of HR Directors (HRDs) today needs to be considered.

The research available from organizations, such as the Chartered Institute of Personnel and Development (CIPD), and the work of respected academics, such as David Guest at Kings College and Chris Brewster at Henley Management College, do not suggest that HR is making a convincing case for taking its seat on the Board. The UK has one of the lowest levels of HRD representation on company Boards or executive groups in northern Europe: in the Nordic countries typically 60–80 per cent of companies have HRDs on the Board. In the UK and Ireland that falls to just over 50 per cent.[12] More worrying is the fact that the same study found that only just under 60 per cent of UK organizations had a written HR strategy. Whilst this was one of the better proportions of the European countries studied, it suggests that the thought process of aligning HR strategy with corporate strategy has not taken place in the UK.

If HR seeks to support the business in its strategic objectives, then defining and documenting an HR strategy seems the minimal entry requirement to join the strategic debate in the boardroom. Should the HR function not already have a boardroom presence, a documented strategy would provide an opportunity for it to raise its profile and set out its stall. Establishing the metrics and tools that enable their HR strategy seem to be even further from the consideration of many HR leaders, since a significant proportion of them have not documented their actual strategy and understood its relationship to the business's strategy.

Why is this happening? In a recent study of the career paths for HRD in the public and private sectors three routes which allowed them to get to the top were identified[13]:

- vertical – the traditional straight route rising through the HR function

- zig zag – starting in HR, moving to other functions to gain broader experience and then returning to HR

- parachute – no previous HR experience before the HRD role; such people are often placed there by the Chief Executive Officer (CEO).

---

12   Brewster, C., Holt Larsen H. and Mayrhofer, W. (2000) 'HRM: A Strategic Approach', in Brewster, C. and Holt Larsen, H. (eds) *HRM in Europe: Trends, Dilemmas, and Strategy*, Blackwell.
13   Kelly, J. and Gennard, J. (2001) *Power and Influence in the Boardroom: The role of the Personnel/HR Director*, Routledge.

The percentage of HRDs who followed each path was as follows:

- vertical – 35 per cent

- zig zag – 57 per cent

- parachute – 8 per cent.

There were differences between the public and private sectors in the numbers taking each path. In the public sector the vertical route was the most common. The predominance of HRD who had experience outside of HR is encouraging in the light of the issues previously described (of HR being too constrained by its view of its role in terms of administration and process). A model for HR in which it is able to interpret and support the delivery of the business strategy requires managers who have a wide range of experience to interpret and anticipate that strategy. They can then assess the impact of HR interventions on the business with greater confidence than colleagues from more traditional and narrower HR backgrounds.

A reasonable majority of HRDs seem to be developing a broad base in their career paths via the zig zag route. They seem to be gaining exposure to other business areas that should be driving their strategic overview and building credibility with other managers. To understand some of the challenges the traditional HR career presents to an HR professional looking to make a strategic impact, the HR specialisms that these directors had covered is revealing, and the same survey found that HRDs had the following backgrounds in HR areas of specialism:

- generalist – 44 per cent

- industrial relations – 35 per cent

- other (for example, learning and development) – 21 per cent.

This is an interesting split because the background of such a large proportion of HRDs is grounded in industrial relations and generalist HR. Typically both are reactive areas of HR. The industrial relations fire-fighter, called into defuse conflict behind closed doors, is a role HR professionals will be familiar with. The HR generalist policeman, interpreting HR policy and legal requirements for the line manager, is also familiar. It is one for which the profession is well prepared by the Chartered Institute of Personnel and Development professional qualifications. Yet neither of these has at its heart the need to develop a vision and strategy for people management within an organization that is aligned with the business's strategic goals. The functions that do drive organizational change and require strategic analysis of an organization's current and future capability and objectives, such as Management and Executive Development or Organizational Design, just do not have any prominence.

A number of studies and commentators have pointed to the constraining nature of the generalist and industrial relations role of HR has on its strategic thinking.[14] This raises a clear question: can a career as a generalist HR manager develop people for the kind of senior strategically orientated HR roles that CEOs are looking for?

SHIFTING THE FOCUS – WHY SHOULD CHANGE OCCUR?

In a recent annual survey of senior HR professionals the respondents identified the major objectives for their HR strategies, where they existed, as:

1. Improve communications between management and employees.

2. Encourage team working.

3. Engender employee commitment and understanding of the business.

4. Control labour costs.

They also identified that little emphasis is placed on:

5. Establishing clear links between pay and performance.

6. Encouraging creativity in the workforce.[15]

Objectives 1 and 2 are certainly enablers in creating the right environment for employees to have good relations with one another and their management, and are a very valid outcome. Nonetheless, it is questionable as to whether they are focused on driving organizational performance. Objectives 5 and 6 seem to be the most focused on driving improvements in business performance. They are arguably the objectives that have the most significant impact on business performance when considering how 'human resources' should be focused, developed and deployed.

Senior HR managers in large organizations in the late 1990s identified that their organizations are most effective in improving organizational performance when tackling issues such as change consulting, merger and acquisition evaluation, improving productivity and bringing new products to the market, shaping the organization's capabilities and its design, and aligning these with the business's strategy.[16] In the light of their views (and the fact that the development of clear pay and performance linkages and the encouragement of workforce creativity are not seen as

14   Lawler, E. and Mohrman, S. (2000) 'Beyond the Vision: What Makes HR Effective?', *Human Resource Planning*, pp.10–20. Ulrich, D. and Beatty, D. (2001) 'From Partners to Players: Extending the HR Playing Field', *Human Resource Management*, Winter.

15   Bevan, S., Cowling, M. and Horner, L. (2004) *Workplace Trends Survey*, The Work Foundation.

16   Lawler, E. and Mohrman, S. (2000) 'Beyond the Vision: What Makes HR Effective?', *Human Resource Planning*, pp. 10–20.

essential) seem to confirm that the shift in HR's thinking towards a function that focuses on delivering the business's strategy and performance is not yet deeply embedded.

This view is reinforced by the work completed by a major consultancy in evaluating the strategic landscape for the pharmaceuticals sector meant for the HR professionals in 2001.[17]

The Future of Pharma HR, predicted that the key areas that would drive the performance of pharmaceuticals companies in the following five years were:

● Organizational design – orientating the Research and Development functions to the challenges that the markets had in store, coping with managing external research collaborations and building cross-border relationships in-company.

● Mergers and acquisitions activity – supporting some of the largest mergers and acquisition transactions that the stock markets had ever seen, from managing exit and knowledge capital retention and organizational integration.

● Creating the right reward schemes – developing individually tailored reward schemes that reward specialist knowledge, which holds the key to product development success in this sector.

Much of the comment provided by CEOs and Managing Directors (MDs) of public and private sector organizations is based on gut-feeling or anecdotal evidence. Whilst there are notable exceptions, HR professionals typically do not provide a robust model for evaluating their input to executing the organization's strategy and objectives. In a recent survey of leaders of large global organizations, only 13 per cent of respondents stated that their CEOs/MDs were very satisfied with the progress their companies have made on their HR initiatives.[18] It seems that in the absence of any powerful data from HR proving that it is having an impact on business performance, senior managers are drawing very unfavourable conclusions about the value HR is creating in their organizations.

And yet HR departments in key sectors are increasing in size at a time when organizations are being asked to respond to pressures to reduce costs in their back-office functions (HR, finance, marketing, and so on). Where these functions are not

---

17   Arlington, S., Delany, K., Dempsey, J. and Matthews, J. (2001) *The Future of Pharma HR*, PriceWaterhouse-Coopers.
18   Cheese, P., Brakely, H. and Clinton, D. (2003) *The High Performance Workforce Study*, Accenture.

perceived as making a powerful contribution to the business's performance it is likely that rationalization will occur. Where they are making a valued contribution, in a world driven increasingly by global competition, the HR leadership team will still be asked to deliver more for less. If HR is not perceived to be delivering then its continued existence in anything like the current format seems unlikely.

In the last two years the average number of employees to HR staff has fallen in a number of key sectors (see the boxed text below). This is a clear message that HR departments are still getting larger. The more performance pressures increase, the harder it becomes to justify continued investment in HR headcount.

EP-First & Saratoga, produces a wide range of benchmark data on HR activities across global and national boundaries and sectors. One of their key measures of HR efficiency is that of the staff full-time equivalent (FTE) to HR staff full-time equivalent (HR FTE) ratio. Table 1.1 tells a story of increasing HR function size in relation to the size of the companies they support.

Table 1.1   HR efficiency benchmarks: The numbers tell the story

	Median FTE:HR FTE	
Sector	2002	2004
Banking	75:1	67:1
IT and electronics	76:1	77:1
Public sector	98:1	73:1
Utilities	124:1	105:1

These figures articulate the average performance of the respondent companies surveyed. The figures for the top performers (in the upper quartile of respondents) showed falls of a similar nature.[19]

If HR is growing and is not delivering strategic value, then it must be focusing on administration and day-to-day operational delivery. This view has been validated in a recent study of US HRDs in medium to large US companies where it was found that over a three-year period the only shift in time spent on various HR activities (from administration to strategy execution) was an increase in the amount of time spent on

---

19   *HR Index Benchmarks*, Saratoga 2004–05, published 2004. *HR Index Benchmarks*, EP-First & Saratoga 2002–03, published 2002.

the administration and implementation of HR policies.[20] Whilst the respondents stated that they believed they had shifted their focus to the activities of HR partnering and to supporting strategic planning, it seems perverse that they then chose to invest no more time on these issues.

The challenge is to create an HR delivery model that can assess the strategic needs of the organization, develop the appropriate people management interventions and implement them successfully. As the profession looked to move on from the early HRM models of the 1980s one figure rose to prominence in seeking to define a future model for the HR function with a key role at its core that sought to address these challenges: David Ulrich. His model of the HR Business Partner outlined a holistic approach for the HR function used to address these issues. His work lies at the heart of a shift in the profession that affects every aspect, from how HR professionals see themselves to how they interact with the business, to the scope of their roles.

HR BUSINESS PARTNERING – THE MODEL FOR CHANGE

We have explored the reorientation of HR towards delivering the organizational strategy and how it has been found wanting in key areas. Key stakeholders feel the function lacks strategic analysis capability, delivers the basics ineffectively or inefficiently and is unable to address the challenges that the new models of HRM posed. Ulrich proposed a model that gave HR a focus to tackle these issues.

It is from this model that the concept of the HR Business Partner (HR BP) has developed. The term 'HR BP' has evolved to address only certain parts of the original model, but a review of Ulrich's concept and objective is essential if a full understanding of the HR BP role as it stands today and an exploration of the path to implemention are to be achieved.

THE ULRICH MODEL

In his book *Human Resource Champions* Dave Ulrich starts with the question 'Should we do away with HR?'.[21] In the opening of the book he suggests that we may have to if we cannot move the focus of HR from solely what it does (for example, recruiting, training or payroll administration) to how it delivers. This is a vital proposition. Ulrich proposes that HR should select four key areas of activity that, when executed well as a whole, will support HR's position and ability to deliver whatever the challenges that may come along (see Figure 1.2).

---

20 Lawler, E. and Mohrman, S. (2000) 'Beyond the Vision: What Makes HR Effective?', *Human Resource Planning*, pp. 10–20.

21 Ulrich, D. (1997) *Human Resource Champions: The Next Agenda for Adding Value and Delivery Results*, Harvard Business School Press, p. vii.

Future/strategic focus

	Future/strategic focus	
Processes	*Strategic Partner*	*Change Agent*	People
	Administrative Expert	*Employee Champion*	

Day-to-day/operational focus

Figure 1.2   The Ulrich model

He maps out new roles for HR. Each role combines to focus on delivering improvement within the function and within the business (see Table 1.2).

Table 1.2   Linking Ulrich's roles to deliverables

Metaphor	Role	Activity	Deliverable
Strategic Partner	Management of strategic resources	Aligning HR and business strategy	Executing strategy
Administrative Expert	Management of firm's infrastructure	Re-engineering process	Building an efficient infrastructure
Employee Champion	Management of employee contribution	Listening and responding to employees	Increasing employee commitment and capability
Change Agent	Management of transformation and change	Managing transformation and change	Creating a renewed infrastructure

Through this model HR is enabled to tackle the strategic issues by having a Strategic Partner who clearly focuses on them. The Administrative Expert helps to demonstrate that HR is supporting the financial goals of the company by focusing on having an efficient and high quality service. The function is also able to focus on the employee relationship and improving employee capability through the establishment of the Employee Champion role. Finally, the Change Agent role allows the function to meet the challenges of the changing business environment and positioning the business to execute strategy.

Ulrich's model has met with almost universal acceptance amongst the HR profession. It offers an inspirational path combined with the comfort of a rather prescriptive and perfunctory description of how to achieve the model. However, Ulrich offers little in the way of empirical evidence to support his model and there is very little in the way of practical suggestions on how to implement the changes successfully.

HR BPs TODAY

Much recent discussion on the development of the HR BP role has focused on strategic delivery. This view may ignore the holistic approach that is essential to meeting the challenges of the future. The HR BP will need to operate in a number of areas, supported by additional parts of the HR function *and* of the wider business, to take on the challenges described.

HR needs to approach each quadrant of the Ulrich delivery model, one at a time. Each quadrant requires different skills to be effective. Each area must focus on the activities that make it successful. Figure 1.3 aligns the Ulrich quadrants with the new HR roles necessary to succeed in implementing this model.

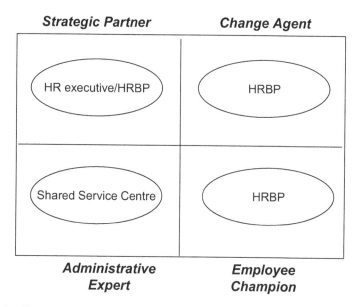

Figure 1.3   Roles in the Ulrich model

Each sector requires a distinct skill set that is considered in Chapter 2. The HR BP alone cannot fill them all successfully. The interaction across the model's elements is an essential element of defining what the core skills, objectives and remit of the HR BP should be. It is from this that organizations can begin to gain a practical sense of what the role of an HR BP actually is.

ROLE OF THE HR BUSINESS PARTNER

Any HR recruitment website or job advertisement tells a story of a rapidly growing trend that indicates, at least on the surface, that the last few years have witnessed a shift away from the more limited aspirations of the generalist HR manager role towards that of the HR BP.

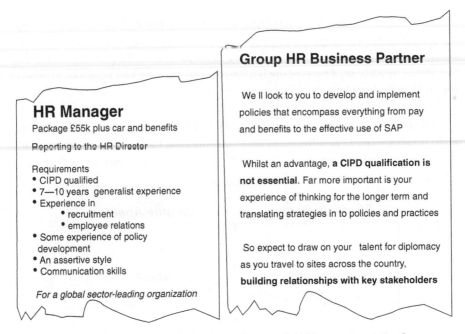

HR Manager
Package £55k plus car and benefits
Reporting to the HR Director

Requirements
• CIPD qualified
• 7—10 years generalist experience
• Experience in
    • recruitment
    • employee relations
• Some experience of policy development
• An assertive style
• Communication skills

For a global sector-leading organization

Group HR Business Partner

We ll look to you to develop and implement policies that encompass everything from pay and benefits to the effective use of SAP

Whilst an advantage, **a CIPD qualification is not essential**. Far more important is your experience of thinking for the longer term and translating strategies in to policies and practices

So expect to draw on your talent for diplomacy as you travel to sites across the country, **building relationships with key stakeholders**

Figure 1.4 A comparison of job adverts for a generalist HR manager and a Group HR BP

The HR BP role needs to be closely aligned with the business. The Group HR Business Partner role in Figure 1.4 involves HR travelling out to business units, developing its understanding of the business's needs and objectives. Whilst there is still the need to deploy a broad range of HR technical knowledge, the key outcome is the effective application of policy advice, influencing skills and deep understanding of how the application of proven technology (in this case an SAP enterprise resource planning platform) can assist the delivery of the business's strategy. The ability to execute this strategy becomes key, rather than the ability just to influence strategic thinking.

Advertised roles typically focus on leaving the roles of Administrative Expert and Employee Champion in the background. The HR BP increasingly relies on other parts of the function (the Shared Service Centre, the Centre of Policy Excellence for example) to deliver the transactional and deep technical expertise of the overall HR functional offering.

This integration across the function of all the available tools at HR's disposal lies at the heart of the HR BP's role and presents some very real challenges for HR. To achieve that it must overcome a number of issues.

The HR BP role needs:

- the credibility to engage with the business
- to be accepted into the management team to allow the HR BP to fully understand the strategic objectives and to influence key decisions with a people dimension
- deep influencing and change and transition management skills than are traditionally associated with HR
- to access the right support, technical and administrative, to enable it to deliver.

These issues point to the contradiction at the heart of the HR BP role; that it is a role that is almost a satellite to the HR function. This has significant implications for staff growing into the role, the development path they choose and, fundamentally, for the future of HR. Chapter 2 takes a look at how companies and public bodies have turned Ulrich's model into a working reality. One that positions the HR BP at the heart of a dispersed HR function, where responsibility for HR delivery is allocated to the most effective point of execution.

This model presents an exciting opportunity for the HR function. An ability to engage in delivering the business's strategy, supported by the credibility associated with the skills of a successful administrative expert is required. The HR BP model can be a means to producing step changes in organizational performance by executing the Change Agent role, supported by the deep understanding of the organization's people that fulfilling the role of Employee Champion provides.

PART 1

The HR Business Partner Model in Practice

CHAPTER 2

The HR BP Role

HR professionals must show how businesses can realise the full potential of their workforces. It's a huge responsibility.

Jonny Taylor, Society of Human Resource Management Board Chair[1]

Having reviewed the theoretical elements of the HR Business Partner model, it is important to look at its implementation on the ground. The last five years have seen very real changes in the activities that HR calls its own and in how the function organizes itself. Practitioners are becoming more familiar with the concepts of Business Partnering, Shared Services and Centres of Excellence.[2] All make a fundamental contribution to the implementation and exploitation of the benefits of the model proposed by Ulrich.

This chapter seeks to identify an holistic model that works. It explores what the HR Business Partner role looks like, explains what senior practitioners see as the key performance indicators and defines the core partnering skills. A detailed case study is used to bring the HR BP model to life.

Recent research (see Figure 2.1) involving the current crop of HR leaders has begun to articulate what the role is about:

'No budget – no resources – the successful Business Partner must be effective at matrix management and in leveraging the service delivery model to best effect ...' HRD, global financial services

'HR mustn't make the mistake of becoming just headcounters, counting heads instead of beans ... business intelligence is what differentiates' HRD, global retail bank

'Letting go – and letting others manage and learn to manage – that's one of the major challenges' HRD, professional services

There are clearly some key themes emerging from these comments.

---

1   Taylor, J C. (2005) 'Courageous HR Leadership', *HR Magazine*, January.
2   Brown, Duncan, Cauldwell, Raymond, White, Kevin, Atkinson, Helen, Tansley, Tammy, Goodge, Peter and Emmott, Mike (2004) *Business Partnering: A New Direction for HR*, Chartered Institute of Personnel and Development.

An HR Business Partner

is proactive

- Acts without guidance
- Initiates and intervenes in ways that add value

is a commercial contributor

- Provides commercial input
- Makes the links between HR and business strategy
- Ensures they have developed an awareness of commercial issues and dependencies

is a leader

- Takes leadership role in cross-functional teams
- Recognizes the difference between leadership and management, but does both

is analytical and an effective user of management information

- Contributes to annual operational plans
- Identifies associated costs and proposes means of addressing them
- Shares the use and interpretation of information and findings
- Understands and utilizes the e-enabled HR tools and is an advocate of the use of e-enabled resources
- Has appropriate skills in basic business packages to perform the role and support their own analytical, presentation and reporting needs

is a champion of the whole HR service

- Encourages cross-activity understanding, working and support
- Participates in wider HR activities – goes the extra mile

anticipates

- Anticipates changes and the implications of changes
- Intervenes early having spotted problem areas and risks
- Evaluates best practice and constantly looks for means of achieving it
- Takes advantage of key learning on review of projects

is well networked

- Establishes and maintains contacts and relationships across business and outside

is results orientated

- Is clear about the limits of authority
- Associates accountabilities with responsibilities
- Has a strong customer orientation
- Leads by example with a positive, personal 'can-do' attitude
- Works to remove any 'blame' culture
- Makes a difference
- Demonstrates resilience

Figure 2.1   Key elements of the HR BP role

- *Deploying resources beyond the HR BP role:* The HR BP role involves the broader HR function. It is this broader function that provides the support the HR BP needs. Knowing how and when to deploy this support is a vital skill for the HR BP.

- *Using business intelligence and analysis:* There is a strong sense that the HR BP can only fulfil their role through robust analysis of the business challenges and an understanding of the impact of these challenges on how people are managed. Analytical skills are an entry-level requirement for aspiring Business Partners. The production of standard HR metrics, such as absence trends, is no longer sufficient to meet internal customer demands.

The questions that need to be answered include 'What do these metrics mean for the business (if anything)?', 'How are they impacting on strategic delivery?' and 'How can the business and HR influence them in a way that helps achieve the organization's desired strategy?'.

- *Learning to manage through others:* Relationship management is another key theme. The HR BP does not have a large hierarchical team to provide them with the organizational status to engage with the business. The HR BP must look to other HR delivery units for the operational support the business needs and must work with non-HR business teams cross-functionally to deliver change. The HR BP has to be capable of managing by evaluating the outputs from its actions and persuading others to act on their behalf. A role with limited direct resources and a desire to be effective can only succeed if one works through others. This involves a need for clarity about the desired results, which makes the initial requirement of accurate analysis all the more important.

These three themes lie at the heart of the role.

LIKELY ATTRIBUTES OF THE HR BP ROLE

The key attributes expected of the person fulfilling the role of HR BP are summarized below.[3]

There is no specific mention in Figure 2.1 of participating in 'core' HR activities such as processing transactions, advising line managers or producing people management reports. The qualities that are listed take the role of HR far more deeply into strategic activities at the company or organization level than is usually found in practice. It is significant that where the HR BP role described in Figure 2.1 lists being results orientated as an ideal attribute, accountability is at its core.

THE HR BP ACTIVITIES IN PRACTICE

A seven-year study of changes in activity for HR where a clear partnering role has been implemented, reveals a series of shifts to strategic planning and strategy execution and delivery. The research shows that the HR BP can expect to spend their time on:

- HR planning
- organizational development

---

3   Orion Partners. Interviews conducted during 2004.

- organizational design

- strategic planning

- management and executive development

- competency/talent assessment

- HR Information Systems.[4]

This confirms the shift in role expectations, rather than the implemented reality, from transaction processing, policy policing and people data report production.

One criticism of this study is that it does not focus on what is being achieved by this shift of emphasis. As a result the research omits to consider how these activities deliver improvements in business performance. A similar criticism can be made of a later Chartered Institute of Personnel and Development study which looked at the same issues.[5]

A MODEL FOR HR BP AREAS OF PRACTICE

The model shown in Figure 2.2 illustrates the working practices of the HR BP – how

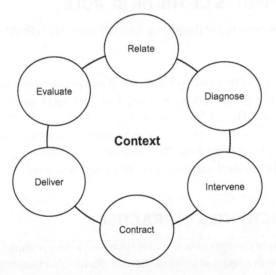

Figure 2.2   The core consulting skills needed to get the HR BP job done

4   Lawler, Edward and Mohrman, Susan (2000) 'Beyond the Vision: What Makes HR Effective?', *Human Resource Planning*.
5   Brown, Duncan, Cauldwell, Raymond, White, Kevin, Atkinson, Helen, Tansley, Tammy, Goodge, Peter and Emmott, Mike (2004) *Business Partnering: A New Direction for HR*, Chartered Institute of Personnel and Development.

they are getting the job done. The model shows how every HR BP activity should be driven by the needs of the business. Fundamental analysis of the business issues and HR's impact upon them is the starting gun for all HR BP work. Evaluating success is the finish flag.

Within the context of the organization's operating environment and strategy, the HR BP covers the following areas:

Relate

The HR BP

- engages with line management and views them as a client
- talks their language
- demonstrates strong commercial awareness and understanding of business needs
- establishes and maintains contacts internally and externally
- helps people share ideas and work across functions
- identifies and manages key stakeholders
- uses a range of styles to influence people and a variety of strategies for approaching them.

Diagnose

The HR BP

- makes effective links between HR and business strategy
- demonstrates awareness of commercial issues and the impact they may have on their role
- identifies the implications of commercial issues for people and the organization
- applies strong diagnostic and analytical skills
- challenges 'client' thinking and perceptions
- identifies external trends and pressures for change and is able to incorporate them in the business's strategy.

Intervene

The HR BP

- influences and shapes the change agenda
- identifies critical business issues and anticipates the people management interventions required to address them
- develops structured recommendations and strategies for implementation
- advises on the cost implications of business strategies
- identifies obstacles to change and develops strategies to overcome them
- helps everyone learn from previous experience, as they go forward.

Contract

The HR BP

- identifies benefits to the business and quantifies the value created by change
- contracts the scope, deliverables, timetables and resources for projects with clients
- ensures expectations are clear and service standards are agreed
- identifies and involves appropriate people and resources to deliver the projects.

Delivers

The HR BP

- delivers agreed outputs
- understands and applies project management methodologies
- coaches others in business changes tools and techniques
- initiates and ensures appropriate communication
- identifies and escalates risk to stakeholders (thus making risk transparent) to ensure they are able support delivery
- organizes their time to work across multiple activities
- places a focus on realizing benefits.

Evaluate

The HR BP

- sets and monitors performance against clear milestones

- encourages continuous improvement using benchmarks for evaluating performance

- quantifies business value of services/outputs delivered, using appropriate financial and non-financial analysis

- oversees related programmes identifying synergies and leveraging benefits

- ensures that the organization learns from successes and failures.

This approach represents a deep shift in the focus of most HR practices. The move is away from inputs (processing administrative tasks) to focusing on the outputs of HR (the impact on the people performance of the organization). The HR BP is not acting as if in an 'ivory tower'. A successful HR BP will understand and align their role to the commercial needs of the business, lead the business to deliver HR services that will achieve these needs and build their credibility in the way they involve and work with others. The aim is to enable the HR function to service managers, employees and the business itself.

ORGANIZING THE TEAM

The attributes and activities of the HR BP are different from those of the traditional HR management role, and an examination of the standard HR hierarchy reveals that the organization of the HR BP team is different too. HR functions have traditionally been aligned along a hierarchy that emphasizes functional specialisms and encourages separate and independent HR service delivery teams developing in each business unit as shown in Figure 2.3.

This traditional model presents a number of challenges for the HR BP model's successful delivery of the HR BP role:

- HR's reporting lines are only HR focused and have limited involvement with the management of the business units they support.

- There is limited opportunity to consolidate administration activities and thus improve service, generate opportunities for investment and free the HR team to focus on the strategic activities previously discussed.

- Sharing knowledge on HR best practice across business units is restricted as HR teams focus on the business unit to which they are aligned.

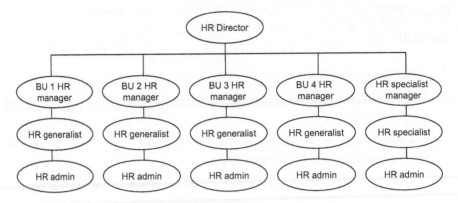

Key: BU = business unit; admin = administration

Figure 2.3 A typical traditional hierarchy for HR

- Business access to HR's experience is restricted to the HR teams that act in the silos serving each business unit.

- Policy implementation is complicated and slowed by the disparate HR processes that tend to evolve in each silo team.

Presented with these challenges the HR function needs to realign its organization with its strategic intent. Figure 2.4 shows a summary overview of the model adopted by the Royal Mail as part of its recent move to implement an HR BP model.[6]

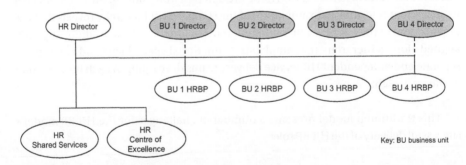

Key: BU business unit

Figure 2.4 The HR BP-based organization structure

This new model embraces the key elements of a new organizational role for HR. It provides solutions to the challenges described above.

6   Brown, Duncan, Cauldwell, Raymond, White, Kevin, Atkinson, Helen, Tansley, Tammy, Goodge, Peter and Emmott, Mike (2004) *Business Partnering: A New Direction for HR*, Chartered Institute of Personnel and Development, p. 28.

- The most senior HR leader, provides a direct link to the group board – allowing for the overall alignment of HR with business strategy and its execution.

- Senior HR managers are directly aligned with the leadership of each business unit as HR BPs – they have a dotted, if not solid, reporting line to the business unit leadership, allowing the closest relationship between HR and the business.

- HR administration is concentrated in a core Shared Services function – this encourages a focus of investment in processes and technology and the adoption of a standardized approach; it also allows policy to be implemented quickly and effectively.

- HR specialists and experts are working together in a Centre of Excellence – this creates a pool of knowledge the business can exploit and through which it can share innovation.

The new organizational model is not without its dangers. Russell Martin, HR Director at Prudential UK, notes that the issue of preventing the HR BPs 'going native' is key[7] because if they do so the HR function begins to lose its integrity of strategy and thinking. This also represents a real risk in that it can be viewed by employees as compromising the role of HR as 'Employee Champion' since HR becomes too closely aligned with 'management'. In certain sectors such as the public sector this can be highly undesirable.

SUMMARIZING THE HR BP ROLE – KEY SUCCESS FACTORS

In reviewing the HR BP model in action, a number of success factors emerge:

- *Learn the business inside out:* If HR is going to be aligned with the business to the point of working alongside and reporting to senior business unit leadership, it has to know that business in detail. This means financially, operationally and strategically. The development of people management solutions and the building of credible relationships that deliver change depend on it.

- *Build great and diverse relationships:* Getting to know the business means getting to know its key players: not just the obvious leaders but also those who are able to support and deliver change and who can provide information that will give the HR BP a deep understanding of how HR might support the execution of the business strategy. Without the advantage of a

---

7   Orion Partners. Interviews conducted during 2004.

large team of direct reports, the HR BP needs to know whom to work with and how to get the job done.

- *Be at the leading edge of the business's thinking:* Credibility will only come from knowing and, more importantly, anticipating the organization's direction and interpreting its future requirements in terms of people. This understanding provides the impetus to devise the right HR strategy and carry it out.

- *Define, track, report and celebrate successes:* Understanding the right metrics is a core skill.[8] This is one of the key ways in which strategies are successfully implemented. There is a strong correlation between the use of processes to measure HR's impact on the business and the existence of HR BPs.

The Pharma Co case study below provides an example of how all these ideas can work. The company adopted an HR BP model and was able to demonstrate deep business understanding, build credibility and then deliver and evaluate change.

CASE STUDY: Pharma Co – the HRBP in action

Pharma Co is one of the largest pharmaceutical outsourcing organizations in the world. Its services include research, medical marketing, information technology and consulting services. With global revenues of US$500m a year and a US stock market listing, its operations are located throughout North and South America, Europe and Japan, covering 40 countries in all. With around 50 per cent of its revenues coming from outside North America, it represents a complex knowledge-based organization whose success is driven by its human assets.

Pharma Co's HR function is led on a global basis by the Global Vice-President of HR (VPHR) with the in-country operations led by two HRDs based in the US and UK. Under the leadership of one of the two HRDs, Pharma Co are implementing the HR BP model in the UK and northern Europe. With a small, focused Shared Service team in the UK for northern Europe, the HR BP model is being deployed as HR staff are freed from their administrative role. With the overall direction set by the Global HR BP, the regional HR team is seeking to change its ways of working within a tight HR budget that is largely held by the business.

The Associate HRD in the UK recounts how members of the team are repositioning themselves with the business to deliver improved services. She says, 'Do not call yourself an HR Business Partner if it means nothing. It is down

---

8   These issues are explored more fully in Chapter 12.

to your name and personal credibility to make it work.' The HR BP roles are project focused and exploit opportunities that are often sought out by HR themselves, as is shown in this following example.

At one of the UK clinical testing units a member of the HR team was able to achieve a significant success, through the HR BP role. The business unit was run by a technical rather than business manager. It was not meeting its performance objectives. By working independently at first from the senior manager, the HR BP was able to assess the key factors affecting the unit's performance using traditional business analysis skills. Once the HR BP had identified these factors the appropriate HR interventions could be defined.

At this point the HR team did not go immediately to the business unit leader. The Associate HRD recounts how they spent many hours building the 'right' to engage the individual on this, through preparatory contacts and relationship building. This enabled them to be seen as a credible commentator whose solutions would be seriously considered. Previously HR would not have been acknowledged as being competent to contribute in this way. Once their credibility was established they could offer what was, by their own admission, a 'bold proposition', which once implemented delivered lasting and significant improvement in the unit's performance.

What made the difference that allowed the HR BP to succeed? The HR BP was able to exploit her position of having oversight across a wide span of the business, and was able to put her access to the right managers to good use in sourcing and applying the solution once identified.

Pharma Co's cornerstones of success

- Coach HR staff members with the success stories about those making the role work elsewhere, building confidence in HR and the HR team.

- Reinforce success stories in the business to promote HR's capabilities.

- If the basics (in other words, HR administration) are not being delivered, then the HR BP will have no credibility. Fix the basics before you try to impress at a higher level.

- You may sometimes need to 'disguise' that you are delivering an HR intervention in the new sense, to gain acceptance. Past experiences create barriers.

- Ensure that your senior HR team have a closely shared vision that they are able to articulate in support of each other.

- Make the metrics you use to qualify and promote success mean something – in a high value knowledge-intensive industry cost per hire is not a management issue but time to hire is something every manager feels.

- Have patience: success does not come immediately.

- Do not look solely in HR for people to fill the Business Partner role.

THE HOLISTIC MODEL FOR HR – THE FUNCTION'S STRUCTURE

Whilst the member of the HR team actually out in the business carrying the job title of 'HR Business Partner' may be working to the new model, they cannot succeed on their own.

HR will never be recognized as an Administrative Expert if they are unable to change employees' addresses efficiently or complete the payroll run accurately. If the HR BP is trying to build credibility with the business, but the nuts and bolts back in HR operations are loose and unreliable, then the partnering role will quickly become untenable.

Meanwhile, if HR is to act as an Employee Champion and Change Agent they need to have the technical expertise to deliver these roles. The roles require HR to deploy specialist knowledge of the tools and processes for managing employee engagement and feedback, as well as having the traditional employee relations and industrial relations competencies. Employment law, reward modelling and organizational development and design are the supporting practice areas required here. Those areas of specialist knowledge in HR and, more importantly, the knowledge to deploy them successfully are essential for the HR BP to fall back on if they are successfully to deliver for the business.

It is essential that the supporting structure and organization are built on solid foundations of best practice and proven records of delivery.

The HR BP for a business unit looks to the Corporate or Group HR function for policy direction and framework. Typically the Group HR function will set the reward models, group policies and metrics against which HR assesses their overall contribution to business performance. The Corporate or Group HR function looks to specialists and administrative staff to police and deliver services against the specified policies. The specialists and administrative staff then, in turn, provide their services to support the HR BP in their role (see Figure 2.5).

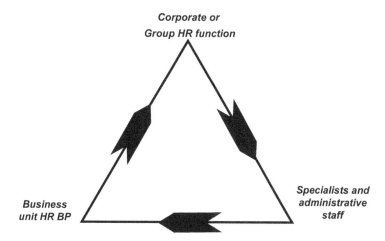

Figure 2.5 The relationship between the HR BP, Corporate HR and the specialist and administrative HR team

Specialists and administrative staff have a key role in backing up the HR BP. Organizations have increasingly implemented a model that seeks to maximize *economies of scale*, in terms of administrative processing through the creation of Shared Service Centres, and *economies of skill* by grouping specialists from across the businesses into Centres of Excellence. These roles and scope of HR activity can been seen in more detail in Figure 2.6.

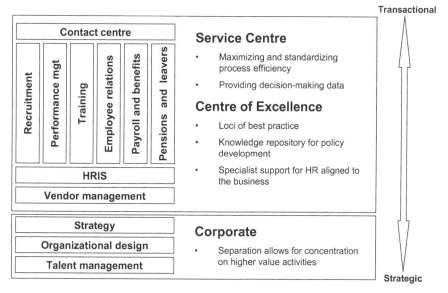

Figure 2.6 The scope of HR activities carried out within the Shared Service Centre, Centre of Excellence and the Corporate Centre

Chapters 3 and 4 examine Shared Service Centres and Centres of Excellence in more detail and Chapter 5 finally considers what can be provided in-house and what should be sourced elsewhere.

CHAPTER 3

The Role of the Shared Service Centre

The Shared Service Centre (SSC) is fundamental to the delivery of the role of HR as Administrative Expert. It provides the focused administrative excellence that drives financial efficiency and HR credibility through the quality of its output, 'getting the basics right, every time'. Whereas the Centre of Excellence (see Chapter 4) is able to provide the focus for the business's expert knowledge on HR, the Shared Service Centre provides a focus for efficiency. SSCs have been able to deliver 20–40 per cent savings to organizations that implement them[1] (the average being at the lower end of the range).

THE SCOPE OF THE SSC

The scope of the Shared Service Centre will be driven by the company's operating requirements and market sector. The key element is that the SSC enables the consolidation of similar HR administration activities from multiple business units. By consolidating processes an SSC is able to control transactional administrative activities better, drive out costs and create a platform for investment in new technologies. SSC staff are judged on the degree to which they can deliver process excellence. The service is delivered through multiple channels, including the Web, telephone and e-mail, to make sure everyone has access to it, when and for what they need it. Face-to-face contact may be possible if the SSC shares the same site or is in close geographical proximity to the employees and line managers it serves (see Figure 3.1).

- *Contact centre:* This forms the principal entry point for customers to contact the SSC. It sits above the process teams handling general queries for employees and line managers. Only specialized or complex queries are referred back to the subject matter experts sitting in the process teams behind the contact centre team. This will usually be by e-mail and telephone. Staff should have sufficient access to information and systems to address user queries and resolve simple actions immediately – ideally 80 per cent of e-mails and calls should be resolved at the first point of contact. The goal of clearing most queries at the first point of contact creates a means to drive

---

1   The Corporate Leadership Council (2001) *Benchmarking Costs in Service Centres*, The Corporate Executive Board, April.

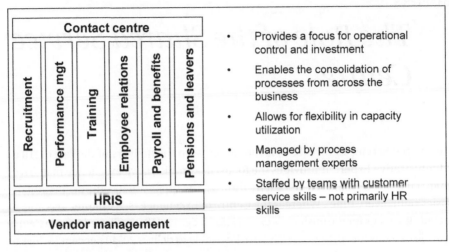

Figure 3.1   The scope of activity for the HR SSC

service improvements for users. HR is available to employees and line managers over the internet or telephone at times that suit them.

The contact centre is also fundamental in supporting the Centre of Excellence and the establishment of HR Business Partners. By creating a first point of contact that is able to filter queries, only those issues that require high-level expert intervention will be raised to the Centre of Excellence staff and only then on to HR BPs.

- *Recruitment:* The teams will be recruiting through CV/résumé management, interview scheduling, early stage interviewing, test centre administration, contract production and on-boarding.

- *Performance management:* Processes managed in the SSC include managing the appraisal round, processing the outcomes into reward mechanisms and notifying appraisees.

- *Training:* The centre concentrates on the administration of training. This may include booking with internal and external delivery providers, scheduling training courses for internal provision, booking venues and curriculum management and updating. The vendor management relationships established by the Centre of Excellence training teams are an important part of working with external providers and venues.

- *Employee relations:* The Shared Services team may be able to offer low-level advice. This may include information on basic processes; it also involves the management of the employee files and data for investigations.

- *Payroll and benefits:* The team is involved in benefits administration. This includes the registration of employees and liaising with third parties to ensure the provision of these benefits. A key role will be the execution of the payroll. This may be only building up the gross pay, which is passed to payroll services supplier, or the full process. Processing of 'Share Save' plans and other reward incentives (bonuses and option-type rewards) may also be administered in the SSC.

- *Pensions and leavers:* Processes executed in this area include pensions administration and the management of pensioner and employee scheme member records. Deductions are advised to payroll and the pensioner payroll run itself where this is not outsourced.

- *Human Resource Information Systems (HRIS):* The teams are mainly involved in data entry, the production of standard reports and a basic level of systems support to the rest of the SSC along a 'super-user' model. Subject to the level of sophistication of the systems much of this should be e-enabled. This is a key way to drive efficiency and savings.

- *Vendor management:* This team focus primarily on the purchase ledger aspect of the HR procurement cycle and vendor performance tracking. Where this activity is not performed by the finance function, invoice reconciliation and tracking will also be executed here.

THE ORGANIZATIONAL DESIGN OF THE SSC

There are a number of essential aspects to the design of the SSC which are summarized below. We go on to the skill sets required to transform the HR functions.

SERVICE MANAGEMENT FRAMEWORKS

A major departure from the traditional HR operating model is the establishment of a means of publicly codifying the service and seeking to govern the standards of its operation through pre-agreed service levels. These concepts may be relevant within the Centre of Excellence, but are more usually found in the SSC.

These frameworks represent a very public shift in HR to a 'customer-centric' service delivery model. The nature of the measures and the amount of resource a company invests in them depend on its intentions for the SSC. The more commercial its operating approach, the more robust tend to be the service measures. Customer charging mechanisms, where they are to be used, also need to be built in here.

STANDARDIZATION

A key concept in delivering the savings from Shared Services is the ability to standardize processes across business units. This is fundamental in allowing the efficient use of resources. The assets of the SSC will largely be people and technology. The easier it is for processes and technology to be used without change across all 'customers', the greater the opportunities of driving efficiency. Standardization will also drive quality improvements. The processes will be simpler and contain fewer inherent opportunities for mistakes.

CENTRALIZATION

Standardization alone will only simplify processes. Centralizing resources and processes will allow the real savings and efficiencies to be realized. Centralization relies on the concept of asset specificity: the less an asset (people, processes or technology) is to a particular operation, the greater the degree to which it can be standardized and delivered across all operations. This will drive up the return on investment in any asset in the Shared Service environment, as the opportunity to use that asset is greatly increased. It is this concept that is fundamental to gaining real value from centralization. Without centralization, HR transformation is simply a consolidation exercise.

An example of a common obstacle to centralization is the different pay processes across each business unit. They may be standardized in each location within the unit, but centralization is the main goal. The assets required to input data, execute the process and produce pay slips for a centralized payroll system can be rationalized to realize economies of scale and flexibility.

TECHNOLOGICAL ENABLEMENT

A key thrust in the development of a Shared Services approach is the use of technology to reduce the effort of processing. This can broadly be split into three approaches. The first uses tools such as the Web and telephone data entry technology to move the ability to perform administrative transactions to the line manager or employee. A commonly cited example is the ability for an employee to change their home postal address on-line.

The second approach uses tools such as the Web and mobile text messaging to keep employees up to date with HR information. Text messaging may be used when staff need to be reminded to complete a transaction. A website may be used to provide a reference point for policy information or to coach staff through a process.

The third approach uses workflow management technology to reduce the amount of human input needed for a process and to speed it up. Workflow technology relies on 'pushing' actions to users when they require completion so, where a job vacancy requires approving before advertising, the system will e-mail the approver with a link taking them to the approval site. Once completed the job will be 'pushed' by the system to the relevant internal job board, internet site or paper media. Whilst this workflow is available within the enterprise resource planning (ERP) packages, it is often expensive to customize it to suit a business's specific processes. As a result stand-alone workflow applications may be used.

CASE STUDY: BT HR Portal (employee self-service)

BT Group have over a number of years developed a sophisticated HR portal for their staff. As users log on they are able to see a user profile that is tailored to their role and position in the company. It links HR policies and processes to life events, such as having to change an address following a house move. An employee can be directed to a section where they can update their address in the HRIS, check holiday allowances to schedule time off to move and complete family and house relocation processes on-line if required.

This approach moves control of the process and some of the effort to the employee. It also uses technology to update databases once and once only. The process is simpler for the employee as they have just one point of reference and do not have to visit numerous parts of the HR department to move through the process.

THE BENEFITS OF THE SSC

The Shared Services model has been successfully developed within a number of functional areas: IT, finance, procurement and now HR. In many ways HR was one of the last to start to reap the benefits of this approach in terms of streamlining its administration. Nonetheless, the benefits it has sought have been the same. Below are some of the commonly cited benefits from implementing Shared Services[2]:

- drives down general and administrative overhead costs
- creates a clear relationship between costs and service
- improves service levels and quality
- maximizes technology investments.

---

2   Quinn, Barbara, Cooke, Robert and Kris, Andrew (2000) *Shared Services, Mining for Corporate Gold*, Prentice Hall.

In some organizations the barriers to achieving the benefits of Shared Services can seem insurmountable. However, many organizations have proven that it can be done and have demonstrated significant benefits through a move to Shared Services in HR.

LOWERING GENERAL AND ADMINISTRATIVE (G&A) OVERHEAD COSTS

Very real cost savings are certainly achievable if the HR function takes a frugal approach to delivering its administration. As a total percentage of G&A costs the contribution of the HR function is often one of the smallest. It is not unusual for HR to cost only 1 per cent of total company net revenue[3]; therefore a 20–30 per cent reduction in these costs delivered by an SSC may be an unimpressive saving in the eyes of the CFO, particularly when the investment in IT or the costs of transition needed for an SSC can be substantial.

The key is not to focus on cost savings alone, but to really understand the value that is created. The HR budget is not the only financial measure (and is a very small measure) of people management's impact on the bottom line and is absolutely no indicator of HR's ability to influence the top line. With the right metrics HR can begin to demonstrate that it may be able not only to operate more cheaply, but also to develop the consolidated information to track its impact elsewhere – for example in tracking and managing employee absence. This will deliver a far greater contribution to the bottom line than the simple savings on delivery costs.

CREATE A CLEAR RELATIONSHIP BETWEEN COSTS AND SERVICE

A highly attractive proposition for any internal business support function is to be seen to be creating a clearly defined set of services that have a clear cost of delivery. Business units can select the services most appropriate to their needs and will accept a change in cost accordingly. In this environment end users are forced to make a conscious decision as to the value they get from a service.

In the past pricing has not always been clear. Businesses are often reluctant to spend time and money developing internal charging structures and schedules that are easy to understand. The same can be said of the requisite service governance frameworks. These instinctively feel like another overhead to manage an overhead. They are, however, essential in ensuring the focus of the SSC is directed at continuous improvement and meeting user requirements.

All too frequently HR does not quantify and track its performance.[4] It is up to the HR SSC to develop performance metrics that go beyond cost and charges to

---

3   *HR Index Benchmarks*, EP-First Worldwide, 2002/2003, published 2002.
4   Cheese, Peter, Brackely, Hep and Clinton, David (2003) *The High Performance Workforce Study*, Accenture.

demonstrate the value and quality they provide. A simple approach is using a balanced scorecard that covers cost and quality and provides improvement targets. User surveys also provide a very valuable means of assessing general satisfaction and setting improvement goals. Involving your customers in such a survey also sends out a very clear message to them that you value their input and requirements and strive to meet them.

IMPROVE SERVICE LEVELS AND QUALITY

Centralized Shared Services and standard processes should make the service provided by HR more consistent and intrinsically easier for its operators to get right every time. Improved process quality is particularly attractive in recruitment and payroll, where mistakes create a disproportionately bad impression of the HR function. Service improvement metrics, on the other hand, may set challenging targets to meet and there are often real barriers to achieving them.

It is difficult to standardize processes across business units. Tradition, 'the way things have always been done round here', unions, employment contract requirements and the genuinely specialist needs of a unit are reasons commonly given for preserving the status quo. Clearly, where a business may have very different needs, allowances will always need to be made. For example, if one part of the business operates a telephone-based customer service and another has highly skilled project-based resources, the recruitment process will need to be different for each.

The key to change lies with a clear business case for doing so and effective stakeholder management. Where standardization makes clear financial sense the business will find it difficult to resist change. Key stakeholders, at all levels, will need to be brought on board to ensure you fight the right 'battles'. If a process is really embedded in the culture of a given department (for example its performance management processes) it may be best left alone and accepted as non-standard.

Work in Shared Services often involves mundane transactional activities and these can lead to employees becoming bored and making errors. Many SSCs have found that job rotation and clear progression through the career structure are essential in preventing this. Job design that builds in variety and gives employees exposure to end users is also a great way to give people job satisfaction.

MAXIMIZE TECHNOLOGY INVESTMENTS

Shared Services can provide a vehicle for realizing the benefits of HR technology investment. The consolidated nature of the SSC provides an environment where technology can support efficient transaction processing. This is particularly true where investment involves consolidating multiple HRIS, implementing ERP systems or building employee Web or telephone access to HR services.

The use of employee self-service and manager self-service technologies to shift the burden of transaction processing onto employees (for instance, as we saw earlier, in making address changes) may only generate small actual cost savings. In addition, processes within companies often need to change rapidly to meet business requirements, which creates the need to redesign any workflow and retrain staff on a regular basis. The real cost of this effort is frequently ignored when the business considers the overall business case for change. Even where the true costs have been assessed and balanced off (the business may be frustrated by the prohibitively high costs of change and blame HR for being a barrier to responding to the market) against the true potential savings the overall organizational effort required to secure these savings may not be judged worth the candle. Inconsistent access to technology can be a problem. Do employees have access to the web or a telephone during their working day? If they do not, the predicted savings will never be realized.

Tackling these issues requires detailed process and workflow analysis to support a business case for utilizing Shared Services. Robust base data of what is actually happening today are needed to justify investment. There needs to be a focus on finding ways to tackle big-ticket costs, not on delivering 'flashy' technology. For example, the investment in Web access for employees to change their personal details may be substantial, but offers little return if few of them actually have web access in their working day. A better approach may be focus on the processes less visible to employees, such as HR entering weekly overtime payments or recording and reporting sickness absence. If these processes are automated via workflow or delegated to line management the savings in HR effort may be very substantial.

CASE STUDY: HR Shared Services in the public sector

Royal Mail – Shared Services at scale

The Royal Mail Group is one of the largest and most prominent employers in the UK. With over 170 000 employees for HR to support, it presents one of the most formidable challenges to administrative HR efficiency.

Prior to the creation of the Shared Services operations, HR was delivered along business unit lines on a regional basis. Each region had its own Recruiting, Training, Pay and Administration team. These teams were running hundreds of legacy databases and applications to manage HR transactions. The need to leverage the benefits of the SSC approach could not have been greater.

As part of the implementation of an internal market and Shared Service approach in all business support functions, HR created its SSC capability between 2000 and 2003.

Organization

HR created three main delivery units employing over 3000 employees.

- Transaction Services – the HR administration operation providing:
  - payroll input
  - employee data changes
  - recruiting administration
  - benefits administration
  - pensions
  - attendance.

- Training and Development Group – the training operation:
  - training strategy
  - training design (often outsourced)
  - training delivery (often outsourced)
  - e-learning
  - assessment centre administration and delivery.

- Occupational Health Services – the health and welfare operation.

Location

The operations were consolidated as below.

- Transaction Services:
  - two main offices in Sheffield and Manchester (each servicing a distinct employee type)
  - four pay input offices, down from 17 after the first phase of consolidation.

- Training and Development Group:
  - three residential training centres.

- Occupational Health Services:
  - one main location in Bristol with satellite offices for seeing employees.

Technology

- Three main large-scale ERP systems, one for each employee group.

- Supported by small local legacy systems to complete specialist activities.

Key points to consider

The Royal Mail's SSC capability shows a very clear grouping around standard processes. This allows the centralization of each regional function's own HR function, driving very significant efficiencies. This also allows for process improvement to be achieved in a more focused and effective way.

With the exception of the pay centres, each location has restricted itself to serving a particular employee group that has distinct process needs. They may all be delivering the same named processes, such as benefits admininstration, but the underlying processes are different due to the employees' terms and conditions of employment. For this reason there is no value in bringing together, say, all the benefits administration processes, as they vary between the types of employees.

There is often 'no one size fits all' for technology. The business has learned to live with the different platforms after they had been consolidated to service only a single workforce. The additional investment in running one single ERP would far outweigh the improvement in processing and data management. They have also recognized that ERPs cannot manage every process. In specialist areas like pensions, legacy applications that have been tailored to the company scheme are far more effective than an off-the-shelf solution.

WHAT IS THE HR BP's ROLE IN THE SSC MODEL?

The model shown in Figure 3.2 was introduced in Chapter 2 as Figure 2.5. In the light of the preceding description of the Shared Services function, the role of each party can now be more clearly defined.

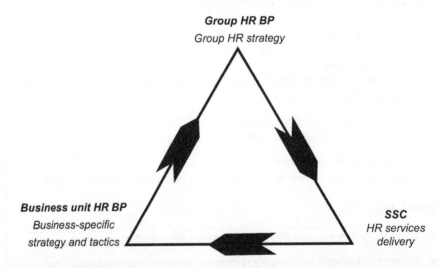

Figure 3.2   The relationship between Group HR, the SSC and business unit HR BPs

Defining where the HR BP role should be focused in relation to the services offered by HR Shared Services is one of the key challenges to implementing an integrated HR model. Figure 3.3 examines a framework within which tasks can be allocated between the SSC and group or business unit HR, to complement and support the HR BP role.

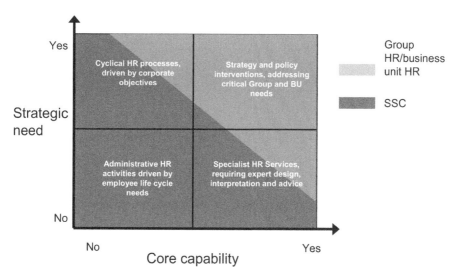

Figure 3.3 The allocation of responsibility for HR roles in the HR BP and HR Shared Services model

The Group HR BP role involves:

- setting strategic HR direction to support the wider business strategy
- scanning the broader environment for best-practice approaches
- determining Group HR policy
- communicating, educating and advising business unit HR and the SSC on the implementation of strategy and policies
- guardianship of HR policies.

The business unit HR BP role involves:

- articulating business unit service needs that align with broader business unit strategy
- providing business specific support on change initiatives, overall resourcing and tactical HR
- providing forecast data on business unit requirements – for example the number of hires, volume of training, and so on
- leveraging business relationships to solve business units' specific issues
- providing Board-level coaching on people issues
- partnering with the SSC to deliver business requirements.

The SSC role involves:

- delivering HR services to business units, line managers and employees
- defining how the service will be delivered to meet agreed business and policy requirements, for example by identifying resourcing channels or managing training delivery and administration
- enforcing the consistent implementation of HR policies
- managing third-party delivery partners, for example resourcing preferred supplier lists
- monitoring and reporting on service quality and customer satisfaction
- identifying service trends to support continuous improvement with the business unit and Group HR.

A failure to define these roles (and allocate responsibility for them) leads to duplication of effort, confusion, unnecessary cost and the undermining of the overall model. If we recognize the need to create a focused administration function, then the HR BPs must leave that transactional part of their role behind. If they do not, the result will be failure to deliver on their part and poor service delivery by the SSC. Each ends up crossing the other's boundaries of responsibility, creating confusion in the eyes of HR's customers and frustration within HR.

CHAPTER 4

The Role of the HR Centre of Excellence

HR BPs need the support of the deep technical knowledge of the business that has traditionally resided in HR. Compensation, benefits and employee relations are areas where specialist knowledge has often evolved within HR teams. The Centre of Excellence (CofE) is the home for these teams; a separate entity, it offers businesses specialist skills and knowledge in particular areas. The Centre also develops and polices policy compliance.

THE SCOPE OF THE CofE

The scope of activities covered by the HR Centre of Excellence will vary according to the nature of HR challenges faced by the industry it supports. For example, in retail, which has high volumes of recruitment activity, those responsible for corporate recruiting policy and programmes will work within the CofE. In the manufacturing sector, teams of employee relations specialists may be based in the CofE and travel to individual businesses when required to provide local face-to-face support and advice. Activities are included in the scope of the CofE if they require deep process and technical knowledge. The types of activity that are typically found within a CofE are shown in Figure 4.1.

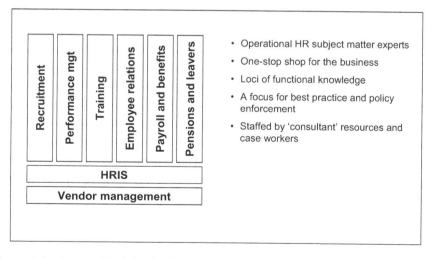

Figure 4.1 Scope of activity for the HR Centre of Excellence

- *Recruitment:* The CofE may include teams of recruiters who support and plan large-scale recruitment programmes and who may deploy to an individual business to support sophisticated selection centres in cases where line managers and local HR BP teams do not have the resources to complete the selection process alone. The CofE teams would manage the corporate recruitment brand – the image and channels through which an employer wishes to be seen in the recruitment market.

- *Performance management:* The CofE also includes individuals who are able to support businesses with policy and design advice as they go through their performance management cycles. This advice covers feedback and appraisal processes.

- *Training:* Training design and training programme management resources may form part of the CofE's specialisms. Delivery resources may also be located in the CofE. External training-provider relationships should be managed by this team to ensure that maximum value is extracted from these third parties. This ensures that these relationships and any favourable commercial and pricing arrangements they may offer are accessible across the whole business. All units within the business can benefit from these arrangements and further advantages can be gained if the business presents a greater volume of business to the third party as a single buying entity.

- *Employee relations:* Depending upon the company's level of unionization, and whether collective agreements exist, the Employee Relationship team in the CofE may focus on managing union relations within businesses. More broadly they will be the team who will support the business in the execution of legal compliance, discipline and grievance processes, and redundancy and sick absence processes, and they will head up the consultation process with both formal and informal employee representatives.

- *Payroll and benefits:* This team will be able to offer business specialist advice on reward policy, payroll, benefits and tax. They would be the group called on to deal with programmes designed to deliver business goals through employee incentive programmes or manage the pay and tax complexities of moving staff around the globe.

- *Pensions and leavers:* The CofE may also offer specialist pension advice. These teams will be operating at a level that is able to support the business in M&A activity and defining pensions strategy. They will also provide businesses with advice on exit policy and programmes and aim to implement early retirement and redeployment initiatives prior to moving to a forced redundancy programme.

- *Human Resource Information Systems (HRIS):* The composition of the HRIS group will depend on where expertise for maintaining the HRIS lies, in either the HR CofE or the IT department. Full technical support may lie within HR or the IT function. At the very least you should expect to find 'super users' of the relevant systems who may maintain structures and user profiles within this team.

- *Vendor management:* The managing of vendors may be integrated within each of the above CofE teams. Since the content knowledge to forge supplier relationships is deep and functional-area specific, it may make sense to locate the vendor management within each team. This team is required to assess the 'make or buy decision' and build supplier relationships to support businesses in achieving the right service levels and service costs. There are frequently very strong links with wider procurement function activities and expertise.

- *Other activities:* It is not uncommon to find that support teams such as occupational health and health and safety are also based within the CofE.

THE ORGANIZATIONAL DESIGN OF THE CofE

The CofE's objective is to formulate and disseminate knowledge and learning around key HR processes to businesses and within the HR teams working as Business Partners. The CofE also defines the policy implemented by the HR Shared Service Centre. The nature of this work means that those working in this area of the HR organization will tend to be formed into teams of project-based resources or teams managing cases of activity, for example a discipline or grievance case that is complex or moving towards the final sanctions of the policy.

An efficient use of expert individuals is to allow them to be seconded on to project teams, managed by the CofE, to support particular initiatives. HR BPs and business customers can call on these resources and the CofE assesses each request and allocates the resources to those projects that it feels, after consultation with the line, are of the highest priority.

CofEs have caseworker staff who work in the areas of discipline, grievance and equal opportunities support. They are able to act as a point of support for line managers, engaging with them and staying with each case as it progresses to conclusion. Because they own the case to conclusion the caseworkers are able to drive the process through and ensure it is conducted in compliance with legal timeframes.

A key part of the CofE's role is acting as a point of escalation for the staff in the SSC for queries that are non-standard, complex or do not have an obvious resolution against current policy. As a result, the business will often contact the CofE initially by telephone or e-mail. Depending on the nature of the case or the project request the telephone call may be as far as the CofE's contact with the business progresses. Where substantial project work or a particularly complex case needs addressing, face-to-face contact is often required; thus CofE teams must be mobile and able to travel to meet their customers.

THE BENEFITS OF THE CofE

Implementing a CofE offers a number of benefits:

- Experience in specialist areas can easily be accessed by the whole organization – it is not just to be found in one site or business unit.

- Learning can be shared across the experts – this drives an overall increase in service quality.

- Greater consistency can be achieved in interpreting policy for the business upon its request.

- Expert staff can be more efficiently deployed – people can work on a project basis wherever the business sees the priority need.

One of the key charges levelled against implementing the new HR model is that the organization loses detailed knowledge about how HR works best in a particular company.[1] The organization's culture and tacit knowledge about how people management activities should be defined and introduced become a casualty as the HR teams get closer to the business and move away from the old world of HR. Against this many might argue this is a benefit in that it allows the speedier adoption of new working behaviours; and any impact of this potential loss of knowledge is counter-balanced by the ability of the CofE to provide a more consistent and controllable service to customers.

Implementing this model can lead to resentment at a local business-unit level, in both HR and the line management communities. Previously HR and the line may have had discretion (welcome by the business or otherwise) to tailor policy and its implementation to the local requirements. These may or may not have been in line with the overall corporate requirements and objectives and frequently undermine the HR function's ability to disseminate good practice and management control. A centralized policy-setting and policing function like a CofE removes that local freedom.

---

1   Trubshaw, Jonathan (2002) *Effective People Management, Helping Authorities Deliver on the 'White Paper' Challenges*, Employers Organization.

Common reward and remuneration practices or standard recruitment processes may, for reasons of corporate identity and operational efficiency, require business units to adhere to a corporate standard set by the CofE. These will be needed despite objections from local business units. Where local flexibility is required, subject-matter experts can be organized to support specific business units and ensure their local needs are met and understood through communication with HR BPs and the local management team. The extent to which local flexibility is balanced against the corporate need for compliance to group policies is one of the key areas of challenge when implementing a CofE model.

WHAT IS THE HR BP's ROLE IN THE CofE MODEL?

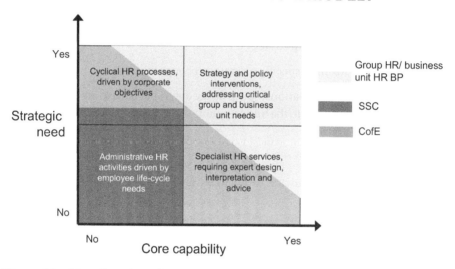

Figure 4.2 The allocation of responsibility for HR roles in the HR BP, HR Shared Services and Centre of Excellence model

The relationship between the CofE and the HR BP role is often complex and is frequently a subject of deep debate when the roles and responsibilities are being defined as part of an HR transformation. There needs to be clearly defined boundaries and the handover points between the roles must be obvious to all. The CofE steps more fully into the role of the subject-matter expert, for example in defining recruiting campaign plans and programmes. It also may plan to take part in the execution or overseeing of some cyclical HR processes, for example annual appraisal or pay negotiations where it might provide specialist advice on how to apply policy for individual managers or aggregating the results from local pay changes and applying expert analysis across business units to provide a company-wide view of trends. To clarify the differences between the Group HR BP, the business unit HR BP and the CofE, these roles are described in detail below and summarized in Figure 4.2:

The Group HR BP role involves:

- setting strategic HR direction to support wider business strategy
- scanning the broader environment for best-practice approaches
- determining group HR policy
- communicating, educating and advising business unit HR and the SSC on the implementation of strategy and policies
- guardianship of HR policies.

The business unit HR BP role involves:

- articulating business unit needs for local policy interpretation that align with broader business unit strategy
- providing business-specific support on change initiatives
- leverage of CofE relationships to apply deep specialist knowledge to solve local issues specific to the business unit.

The CofE role involves:

- delivering expert advice to business units, HR BPs, line managers and employees
- policing the models, processes and policies that will be used to deliver HR to the business
- identifying service trends to facilitate continuous improvement with the HR teams within the business unit and group.

CASE STUDY: The HR BP model in action

Over the last few years Prudential UK has moved to the HR BP, HR Shared Services and CofE model. It currently employs 405 employees in HR serving an employee base of around 7000. The climate of change that often drives the implementation of a new HR service-delivery model was clear at Prudential: rapidly readjusting its cost and base and providing a more responsive HR function were the key challenges.

A review of the model's implementation allows us to see three key aspects of it:

- An holistic implementation of the model brings the greatest benefits.

- The stability and control the SSC brings is unparalleled.

- The business strongly welcomes the closer relationship with HR through their HR BPs.

The model as it is currently deployed at Prudential is shown in Figure 4.3. The elements of the Shared Services, CofE specialist support and HR BP roles are aligned with Ulrich's holistic model for HR activity.

Figure 4.3   Prudential's allocation of Ulrich's key roles to the HR model

The HR BPs are a highly focused group, supported by a geographically mobile, project-based team of specialist support staff. These specialist support teams form the equivalent of the CofE. The specialist support (CofE) at Prudential covers employee relations, resourcing, internal communications and learning and development. They work as virtual teams wherever the business need and project arises.

The SSC is fronted by the ASK HR call centre function that provides the principal point of contact for employees for HR.

The role of technology

Supporting the SSC and ASK HR is the HR intranet which contains the key policies and processes. As Prudential is a predominantly office-based organization this approach works with a PC-literate workforce who have constant access to web pages and e-mail.

Implementation

During an interview with Orion Partners, Russell Martin (HR Director UK) made the following comments about the implementation of the model.

Benefits realized:

- HR transactions are now standard and can be delivered anywhere.

- Staff can be trained to deliver HR transactions to a higher standard and the stability of the processes is greatly improved.

- Recruiting is now handled through the SSC and HR has control of this key process.

- HR targets are measured against Saratoga's benchmark metrics to benchmark performance and set targets for improvement.[2]

- Business managers have come to include the HR BPs as part of their organization structure, demonstrating that the HR BPs truly have got close to the business.

Issues encountered:

- Business Partners have had their budgets withdrawn to ensure they draw on the CofE teams and the SSC.

- A quick implementation period was required to force the pace of change. Five HR businesses were merged into one overnight.

- Over 60 per cent of the operational savings were made from the move to the model and not gained through the deployment of new technology.

---

2   See the *HR Index Benchmarks* published by Saratoga annually.

CHAPTER 5

The Role of Outsourcing

As HR pursues its goal of becoming an administrative expert, it frequently looks to outsourced service providers to further develop this competency.

'Outsourcing' can be defined as the transfer of an internal business function, or group of related activities and assets, to an external supplier or service provider who is prepared to offer a defined service for a specific period of time and at an agreed price.

The use by companies of external third parties to provide services that were previously applied internally is not a new trend. Since the early 1970s the HR function has increasingly looked to source the provision of some of its activities from suppliers who can do the work better and at less cost. The provision of pension and payroll services, relocation and employee incentive programmes and the delivery of training and development activities are just a handful of examples of activities that have an established history of successful outsourcing. The significant change in thinking over the last ten years has been the recognition that the main 'added value' activities performed by the HR specialist have little to do with repetitive, transactional administrative activities and much more to do with strategy and policy. This change of mindset has led to some companies, most famously BP, BT and Cable & Wireless in the UK, deciding to outsource the entire administrative HR 'back office' activities to external suppliers.

WHAT ARE THE ISSUES DRIVING COMPANIES TO OUTSOURCE THEIR HR FUNCTIONS?

There are a number of different pressures and drivers that are encouraging firms to consider seriously taking the outsourcing route. Overall, the factors are often similar to those that encourage the adoption of an internal HR Shared Services model. The particular set of drivers for an individual firm will vary according to the industry and history of the company. However, the following factors are usually found behind any outsourcing business case.

THERE ARE MORE IMPORTANT BUSINESS MATTERS ON WHICH TO FOCUS RESOURCES

The debate over a company's and function's core competencies has led to the identification of a set of activities that a firm must focus on to be successful and a set of activities that are deemed non-core to the business. Research by *Personnel Today* indicated that HR staff spend up to 85 per cent of their time on managing standard administrative processes and only 15 per cent on strategic activities. In best-practice companies these percentages will typically be reversed. By outsourcing these non-core business activities HR functions can focus the managerial effort on delivering the strategic and high-impact policy matters, such as winning the war for talent, which are of true value to achieving business goals. Consequently the time and effort required to manage routine administrative and data management work can be avoided and internal resources can be redeployed to more useful work.

THE NEED TO REDUCE THE COST OF THE HR FUNCTION

The increasing global competitive pressures experienced by almost all large companies, together with the search for synergies following the wave of mergers and acquisitions in the late 1990s, has forced functional leaders to reduce their internal costs. The Conference Board published research in 1999 that showed that nearly 80 per cent of all firms were demanding contributions towards achieving cost reduction targets from their administrative functions, including HR. The tightening economic environment, collapsing stock market valuations and the decline in year-on-year annual growth rates in the first years of the twenty-first century have only made these pressures more acute. To retain credibility with line managers and senior executives the HR leadership team need to contribute to achieving better margins. They need to support competitive advantage by moving to a continuous improvement mindset and by seeking rigorous cost reduction opportunities. HR needs to improve its performance in delivering the basics; that is to say, it must become an administrative expert.

THE NEED TO INCREASE SERVICE EFFICIENCY

A very common driver behind outsourcing is the need to respond to changes in internal customer expectations. Research by the Saratoga Institute (owned by PriceWaterhouseCoopers) has revealed high levels of dissatisfaction with HR service levels. HR has scored typically between 3 and 4 (out of 7) from line managers indicating the need for HR to enhance its service offering.[1] Widely publicized advances in technology, and in particular the spread of eHR direct services allowing the employee and manager to do many administrative tasks on-line, have created pressure on the HR function to consider new more efficient service delivery channels.

ADVANCES IN TECHNOLOGY

The developments in internet and intranet technologies over the last five years have dramatically changed the options for delivering HR services. eHR, as the use of

---

1   *HR Index Benchmarks*, EP-First Worldwide (also known as Saratoga), 2002/2003.

intranets and the internet to improve the effectiveness of a firm's people is commonly known, can have a dramatic impact on both how HR services are delivered and the location of those who deliver the services. The elimination of the need for most hard-copy paper documentation has freed up the HR function to rethink the whole basis of how it delivers its services; a combination of web tools, e-mail, call centres and integrated information systems can now be used to provide quicker access to better information at a time of the user's choosing. HR outsourcers are able to provide access to these proven technologies at a price that is highly attractive to many potential customers.

GREATER ACCEPTANCE OF THE CONCEPT OF OUTSOURCING

Increasingly, many organizations have (more or less) successfully outsourced one or more major process. These positive experiences have made it more acceptable for companies to consider extending the concept beyond the more traditional outsourcing targets (for example, finance, payroll, distribution and IT) to include other functions such as HR where the economics of outsourcing can also be leveraged.

EMERGENCE OF A CREDIBLE SUPPLIER BASE

Companies located in the UK and North America are well served by a raft of proven and competent suppliers of a full range of HR services. Specialist HR outsourcers such as Exult (www.exult.net), Xchanging (www.xchanging.com) and ACS (www.acs-inc.com) provide a full service offering to potential clients together with a group of reference clients who can articulate and confirm the advantages delivered by the outsourcing route. Needless to say these pioneering clients can also provide wise words around the risks and challenges of implementing an outsourced solution. More traditional outsourcing providers, looking to play in the HR space, have joined this group of specialist providers and deepened the choice in the market. For example, Accenture HR Services (www.accenture.com), International Business Machines (www.ibm.com), Rebus (www.rebusgroup.com) and EDS (www.eds.com) have all been active in the HR outsourcing area and have all won clients in the last two years. This arrival of a credible supplier base has been a significant factor in pushing outsourcing on to the HR agenda.

PROVIDING A PLATFORM AND MOMENTUM FOR CHANGE

Companies have also often acknowledged that, whilst they may be able to afford to finance the change, they lack the internal capability, corporate will and need to demonstrate something very radical has happened.

Outsourcers tend to be supported by experienced change management teams who are able to move quickly to implement an outsourcing solution. There is no delay from waiting for internal resources to become free before the programme can begin. The commercial pressure created by the contractual relationship also drives the provider to move as fast as is reasonably possible to get the service operational. In addition, engaging a third party to handle all or large areas of HR process signifies to the organization that things are changing in HR and fast. HR outsourcing is still new enough to signal a step change in direction for an organization.

When Cable & Wireless outsourced the administration of their HR function in 2001, their programme leadership admitted they could not have achieved the change they did without the momentum created by working with an outsourcer.

WHAT ARE THE ADVANTAGES OF OUTSOURCING?

The main advantages of outsourcing that have been identified include the following[2]:

- savings in the time taken to deliver services

- increased organizational efficiency

- clearer alignment around roles and responsibilities for the retained in-house HR team

- greater focus of energy and resources on HR's core business of providing strategic advice and deep policy expertise to business managers

- improvements in the quality of transactional services

- significantly better ability to measure the day-to-day service and productivity achievements of the HR function

- clear success measures and agreed service-level standards make service expectations on both sides transparent

- greater control of the HR function's activities and spend through robust contracts (this can also be seen as a disadvantage)

- better access to state-of-the-art eHR and information systems

- significant reduction in costs (typically greater than 25 per cent)

- increased levels of positive customer feedback.

WHAT ARE THE DISADVANTAGES OF OUTSOURCING?

The main disadvantages of outsourcing that have been identified include the following:

2   Orion Partners. Interviews conducted during 2003–04.

- There may be a dependence on the development of skills in third-party account management which may not naturally exist within the company.

- It may take considerable time for the retained HR function to adjust to focusing on managing 'outputs' from the outsourcer rather than managing the process which delivers the outputs.

- Poorly designed scope of services and ill-defined service levels can encourage inflexible responses from the outsource supplier if not carefully managed.

- The transfer of knowledge to the outsourcer requires effort and dedicated resources which are not always sufficiently costed in the business case.

- There may be a perceived loss of control.

- When outsourcing contracts come up for renewal the outsourcer is normally in a stronger bargaining position than the client organization because of the cost and effort required either to transfer or take back in-house the contract.

- The signing of an outsourcing contract is the beginning not the end of the process. It takes dedicated effort successfully to manage the contract and the issues that will arise on a day-to-day basis as the relationship with the outsourcer beds in.

- If an outsourcer has been tightly screwed down during negotiations to an unrealistically tight budget then it will not be incentivized to put its best people on the contract. Service standards can be threatened if unrealistic prices have been agreed resulting in a lose:lose situation for all involved.

- As the business environment and challenges change for the client organization, the contract with the outsourcer will need to be revised in order to reflect new business priorities and realities. Unless properly set up this change control process can be distracting for both sides of the deal.

CASE STUDY: The typical shape of outsourcing arrangements, Cable & Wireless Global

Cable & Wireless (C&W) is a global communications business providing a full range of telecommunications services to businesses and individual consumers in 33 countries.

C&W was experiencing declining revenues due to increased competition and a softening market. Cost reductions were sought through an HR transformation programme designed to e-enable the HR function, delivering core HR functionality to the manager's and employee's desktop. C&W further maximizing its ability to make its cost base variable.

C&W signed a five-year agreement with Accenture HR Services in December 2001 to serve 6500 UK employees. The original deal also covered the US, but was later withdrawn as business requirements changed.

The scope of HR services provided by Accenture included:

- provision of a one-stop shop call centre for all employee and line manager HR queries;

- recruitment, including administration and contract production (later moved to an alternative third-party provider);

- performance management administration;

- learning and development administration and some intervention development;

- benefits administration;

- employee payroll;

- wage and salary administration;

- employee information services;

- provision of global e-Learning and e-Recruiting applications.

C&W retained in-house:

- HR strategy and policy;

- HR Business Partnering;

- talent management;

- organization design and development;

- provision of SAP global HRIS.

WHAT IS THE HR BP's ROLE IN ANY OUTSOURCING ARRANGEMENT?

The role of the HR BP in outsourcing is in essence very similar to that in working with the Shared Service Centre (see Figure 5.1), though fundamentally this role requires a more sophisticated approach to relationship and commercial management. The HR BP needs to be far more commercially aware of the impact of their requests on the service provider. Often the costs of HR projects, policy or process changes or HR

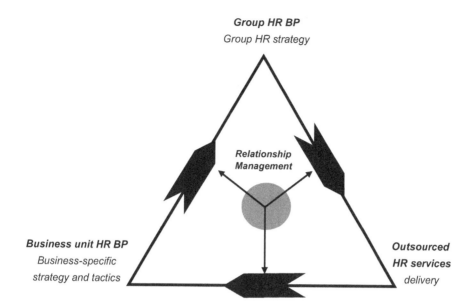

Figure 5.1 The relationship between Group HR, the outsourced function and business unit HR BPs

activity cycles service changes result in a charge from the service provider. These crystallize the costs of HR activity in real cash terms, in a way that internal SSC operations do not.

The following activities for the HR BP become essential if the relationship with the service provider is to have the impact to deliver the intended results and on the supporting elements of the HR model:

- managing the service contract through clearly specified outputs and scope;

- managing and evaluating the impact of business change on the commercial relationship;

- reinforcing the use of the provider to ensure that the most is made of the commercial advantages (that have been negotiated).

Whilst the role for the HR BP working with an external provider may be subtly different from their role within the internal Shared Services model, it is arguable whether HR is sufficiently knowledgeable enough about the skills required to track, measure and manage external suppliers. This is a subject that will be further covered in Chapters 14 and 15.

CHAPTER 6

What Does this Mean for the Line Manager?

If the business is the client for this new triangular HR model of HRSS, HR BP, and CofE, what does this mean for the line manager, who has the most frequent and direct contact with the employees and customers and every day feels the pressure to deliver business objectives?

Much research has focused on the need for line managers to 'own' their people issues.[1] Line managers are closest to the issues and are often the face of the company to their teams. As such it makes a compelling argument for providing line managers with the skills and tools to improve their 'people skills'. A study of the pharmaceutical industry found that employees in this knowledge-intensive industry were more likely to leave a company to follow a good line manager than for more money.[2]

In addition, the intervention of HR in staff relationships with line managers and HR process transactions is often a sign of significant inefficiency in an HR function: HR staff passing CVs on to managers who are recruiting, HR spending time dealing with minor disciplinary issues where the process and facts are clear, HR involved in keeping vacation logs and conducting return to work interviews – these are all common examples of interventions with limited value. It is often quicker and more efficient for HR to step out of the process and allow the line manager to deal directly with such issues.

THE ROLE OF THE LINE MANAGER

The line manager at each management level has a key role to play in delivering the new HR model. The depth and scale of their role varies across each of the quadrants of HR activity as illustrated in Figure 6.1.

The inexperienced line manager is not well placed to act as a Strategic Partner in HR terms. They do not have a deep understanding of the work of the company's

---

1 Hutchinson, Sue and Purcell, John (2003) *Bringing Policies to Life: The Role of Front Line Managers*, Chartered Institute of Personnel and Development.
2 Arlington, Steve, Delany, Kevin, Dempsy, Jo, Matthews, Joanne and Peck, Jonathan (2001) *The Future of Pharma HR*, PriceWaterhouseCoopers.

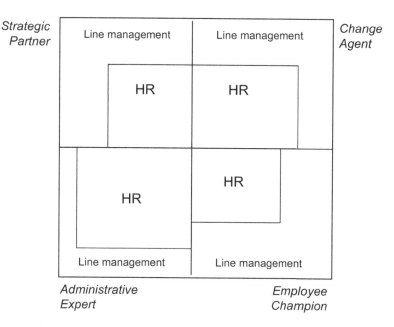

Figure 6.1   The scale of contribution of the line manager compared to that of HR, in each of Ulrich's areas of HR activity

strategy development teams. Their siloed view of the company also prevents them from having a complete view of the resources at the firm's disposal to execute strategy. The senior line management team does, however, have a fundamental role as a Strategic Partner, by signing off (at executive and business unit leadership level) the HR strategy the business will be taking. Indeed, the HR leadership team can only define this strategy by developing a partnership with the senior management and executive team.

Line managers will take only a limited role in ensuring that HR is an Administrative Expert and is able to operate and run an efficient function. They can contribute by signalling requirements and by approving the models and approaches HR uses to deliver an efficient service.

The role of Change Agent presents a greater opportunity for the line manager. HR can be the instigator, facilitator and owner of people issues in change programmes, but the line managers are often the delivery vehicle for change and owners of the overall outcome.

It is the role of Employee Champion that is potentially the area in which the line manager can make the greatest contribution. Line managers have a close relationship with their employees and a level of day-to-day contact that provides the potential for deep understanding of employee attitudes. A clear sign that line management is listening to and engaging with employees will improve employees' satisfaction significantly.[3] The line manager has access to the information that can inform, guide and confirm HR strategy, policy development and business change.

THE LINE MANAGER'S CONCERNS

By moving what may have been previously seen as 'HR activities' to the line, a number of issues are likely to be encountered. More often than not these are raised by line management themselves.

SKILLS

Much has been made of the need to raise the skills of line managers, particularly at the first-line level. Line managers are often in their positions because they possess technical knowledge about their field of operations, rather than because of their people management skills.

Developing these human skills involves increasing their knowledge of HR policy and process and improving their people management skills.

Increasing their knowledge should not be an attempt to instil the entire HR handbook in the line management community. Line managers only need the basics to ensure legislative and company policy compliance. What they will need is the right level of expert support, provided through either an HR Centre of Excellence or a Shared Service Centre.

Developing the skills of line managers involves identifying their skill gaps. In the longer term it makes sense for these skills to be part of the core skills or competencies of line management that the business selects and recruits to.

COMMUNICATIONS

In any programme of change, communications is a key area. Line managers must understand clearly what their role is, where they can get support and why a specific change is happening. If these are not communicated and understood the change will fail.

In certain HR roles, for example Change Agent and Employee Champion, the line manager has a significant responsibility. If they do not have a clear view of the change

---

3   Holman, David (2002) 'Employee Well-being in Call Centres', *Human Resource Management Journal*, Vol. 12, issue 4.

programme and its objectives and are not equipped with the skills to deliver the change, they will not be prepared or able to deliver. Line managers need the skills, process support and voice within the organization to be able to fulfil the role the model demands of them. Without these they will quickly feel disempowered and unable to meet the challenges and where this happens HR will find itself pulled back into the vacuum where activities it believed it had passed to the line managers had once been.

VALUE

HR is just one of the business support functions that is looking to boost the role of line managers in delivering its services to employees. A range of other functions is expecting the line manager to take on additional tasks that used to reside in them. For over ten years IT departments have been asking employees and line managers to take on activities such as updating applications and installing software, moving the onus for problem resolution onto the individual to reduce costs. Finance departments have been moving more of the role of approval and tracking to the line managers to enable them to focus on the core activities of financial management and planning. HR may just add to this burden. If the line managers cannot see any benefit in stepping up to take this work on, then they are unlikely to do so.

There is little value in HR just pushing work it used to complete itself onto line management: this will cause resentment and damage the credibility of HR. There needs to be some degree of transformation that enables the line manager to see that doing the work is of value to them, their employees or the organization to ensure take-up. Using technology to e-enable basic administration or reporting, for example entering overtime payments, is one example of how technology can be seen to benefit line managers. By 'e-enabling' transactions (executing them through on-line applications) employees and line managers gain the ability to undertake HR transactions at their convenience, using the HRIS directly. This is often provided by self-service applications in systems such as SAP or Oracle. Paper forms that need to be found, completed each time and sent off are replaced by an on-line service. Other methods to improve administrative efficiency include process re-engineering, for example all sickness absence could be reported directly to a central HR SSC, which can then manage the tracking and reporting of sickness. This example also creates significant value for the organization. It can now take a corporate-wide view of sick absence, quantify the cost of the problem and develop measures to control it.

REVIEWING THE MODEL

The HR BP model represents a significant departure for HR. It demands skills that move HR from its traditional comfort zone. New operating models for managing the transactional processing and specialist elements of HR require new management skills, as well as raising the profile of the function and its specialists. Interaction and alignment with the business creates the need for an understanding of the organizational issues, politics and people that HR has never needed before. The HR BP must execute their role drawing on a number of ways of working and relationships that have not been a central part of the traditional HR manager's role and experience.

The role of a range of actors within and external to the organization is far more dynamic than merely the function itself and essential to the delivery of HR's objectives. HR has to recognize that it is not best placed to do everything that is 'people' related. External providers may bring something to the function's capability that cannot be ignored. Once HR has focused on how it will deliver the organizational objectives and support its people in doing so, it can reach out to those best placed to help it deliver. The line manager is a crucial arm of this delivery. Indeed, line managers are often crying out for the opportunity to manage their teams with professional, empathetic support from the 'people management experts', HR. With the support of an HR BP the line can be empowered to deliver its strategy and operational objectives.

It is clear that 'less time on administration means more time on strategy', and defining what this 'strategy' is and how HR engages in the strategic debate is fundamental. The challenges of defining what the activities are that support the organizational strategy and how they can be evaluated are the key themes that shall be explored in Chapter 12.

PART 2

HR Technology – the Business Partner Toolkit

CHAPTER 7

The HR BP and Technology

All of the HR Directors and Business Partners approached by Orion Partners as part of our research for this book regarded HR technology as being a key enabler of the core components of their strategy. Employee and manager self-service were frequently cited as the technology components likely to have the greatest influence on future delivery models for HR. Indeed, without the assistance of new technology in redesigning the way that work is managed within the HR function and allowing the delivery of service from remote locations, the HR BP model will be an organizational non-starter.

There are significantly different views on how technology should be deployed and what its true value and business benefit is to the organization.

Different experiences of HR technology

Oracle: Unsurprisingly for a technology vendor, Oracle are enthusiastic in describing their success in integrating self-service and workflow capabilities into everyday HR transactions. Oracle have automated to such an extent that, for major operations in the Europe, Middle East and Africa region, no significant investment is required in HR administrative resources. As a result an overall HR to staff ratio of 1:250 is maintained in the region even though the organization operates in 34 separate countries.

Prudential UK: In the last two years Prudential has significantly reduced HR costs and implemented new service delivery models including an HR Shared Service Centre to manage administration for 7000 staff. However, most of this change was executed in advance of investment to replace their dated mainframe HR technology and this suggests that the technology is not the major driver of cost savings.

TUI: The Thomson Holiday/Lunn Poly group are in the process of managing the HR implications of their merger and have tackled the issues of consolidating administration and setting up HR BPs. TUI has identified an urgent need to invest in technology as a driver for improved service delivery models in HR. However, in a cost-constrained environment, the case for investment will only be made on the basis of proven hard benefits.

For the HR BP seeking to act as a business-based HR expert, technology is a critical tool to support delivery and will govern their access to:

- critical HR management information to support business decisions
- specialist data to support planning and development
- the transactional service provided by an SSC or outsource provider.

Common themes relating to the problems of legacy (old, semi-redundant) HR systems were cited by most of the organizations we spoke to. These problems were said to be serious constraints to the operational effectiveness of HR and the delivery of HR's strategic objectives.

Commonly diagnosed HRIS problems

- Fragmentation of technology platforms and lack of a common source of HR data lead to poor data quality and inconsistent and inaccurate management information.

- Lack of integration between core administration processes and IT systems lead to inefficient practices such as double keying of data, excessive manual checking of results and manual compilation of statistics.

- High paper content and use of paper-based forms in most HR processes.

- Disparate technologies and processes constrain the ability of the organization to rationalize or consolidate operations.

- Complex or risky operations around critical applications such as payroll.

- Proliferation of isolated stand-alone applications.

- Prohibitive cost of investment in new applications – difficult to identify hard benefits to justify cost.

Although the Business Partner may not carry responsibility for the delivery or management of technology, HR systems form a critical part of the environment in which they work and can radically alter their chances of success. If the HR function is unable to resolve the technological challenges of getting the basic administrative services delivered effectively then it is unlikely to be able to get much traction with senior managers around the concept of delivering a partnering service.

To be effective, it is vital that an HR BP understand the potential of HR technology and the mechanisms by which it is delivered successfully. Only with this knowledge can the Business Partner ask the right questions and make the right demands of those who provide their technology support.

WHAT DO HR SYSTEMS HAVE TO OFFER?

There is a strong temptation at the start of any project to jump into a comprehensive vendor selection exercise; this provides the twin satisfaction of being able to look at the goodies on offer and also creates the illusion that the project is moving forward. However, without an understanding of the strategic context in which the system will operate, the HR BP runs the risk of investing time, effort and money in technical dead ends that will not deliver the functionality and information for making a proactive contribution to the business.

CORE ELEMENTS OF A HUMAN RESOURCE INFORMATION SYSTEM

A good place to start involvement in an HRIS project is to develop a familiarity with the bewildering array of applications and add-on modules on offer from software suppliers. Developing an early understanding of this terminology and what the components of an HR solution offer will help the HR BP to make informed choices about the relevance and potential benefit of any particular solution and could help avoid early project mistakes.

The following is a generic checklist of the typical components of a modern HRIS with a brief overview of their functionality. It will serve as a guide to what is being offered and what may be needed to support the functional scope.

CORE HR APPLICATION

In general most of the major package suppliers will provide a core module to support HR records from which other applications in the business can draw their data. The precise functionality offered by the core application varies significantly between suppliers and may include services related to recruitment, training, recording working hours, compensation, and so on. This is often supplemented by functionality from specialist modules (see below).

RECRUITMENT/TRAINING/TIME AND ATTENDANCE

Dedicated modules are frequently added to the core application to support more comprehensive requirements in specialist areas of HR. The specific functionality of these modules varies but may include components of web-based access for vacancy posting, recruitment applications, training administration and time and attendance.

The range of modules offering add-on functionality has grown significantly in recent years and may mean different things to different suppliers. For example the concept of 'learning management' covers a range of functionality from simple training administration to, in some instances, competency management, course catalogue publishing and eLearning applications. Project owners are well advised to check the functionality contained in an offering to ensure they only buy what they need.

PAYROLL

Although not covered in depth in this chapter, payroll is frequently considered alongside requirements for new HR systems and may be considered as part of an integrated package. Essentially this means that payroll will operate from the same employee database as the core HR application and this will remove the need for complex interfacing and eliminate the duplicate data entry which frequently occurs when legacy operations with poorly interfaced HR and payroll applications are used. This is an essential requirement if the HRIS is required to support a Shared Service operation for HR where payroll process will be managed as part of an integrated service.

REPORTING/ANALYTICS

Approaches to reporting may vary with different suppliers of systems. Whilst some reporting capability is usually available as part of the core module more comprehensive tools are often available separately. Third-party reporting products such as Business Objects or Cognos may also work with the package and may already be familiar to the organization.

The concept of HR analytics has grown significantly in the last few years. Whilst reporting tools focus on historic data and report past events, analytics tools attempt to focus on trend forecasting in order to highlight areas requiring management attention. Such an approach can be very powerful when combined with a balanced scorecard approach to defining and monitoring key performance indicators in HR, although there is a significant overhead in setting up and maintaining such tools.

SELF-SERVICE AND WORKFLOW

Self-service capability is frequently sold as a separate module and refers to the facility that allows non-core users of the HR system access to HR data and transactions. The level of such access might be as basic as employees updating a change of address or it may involve a line manager as an integral part of the HR processes of resourcing, payment, performance management and termination.

Similarly, 'workflow' refers to the capability to define and automate a process allowing certain 'triggers' to initiate follow-on actions through the use of e-mail, reminders and designated system actions. A typical use of workflow might be the entering of a new employee's record into the system, triggering a number of related actions such as notifying security of the need for a pass, enrolling the employee on induction courses, notifying a line manager of their start date, and so on.

Self-service and workflow are increasingly core elements to the delivery of new HR service models. The ability to devolve parts of the HR process to the line and to automate processes where possible is a key driver behind the move to Shared Service operations and the benefits that come with them. Similarly, HR outsource providers can use these facilities to manage client services and systems remotely.

However, self-service features are not a universal panacea for organizations proposing to transform HR. Many organizations cannot take advantage of these solutions for a variety of reasons, for example:

- Technical architectures may not possess the bandwidth to manage self-service transactions via the web (particularly where multiple locations are involved).

- Workflow systems may carry a significant overhead for HR because they need an organization to have a hierarchy that can drive the authorization of self-service activities. Organizations that do not currently maintain detailed organizational structures may be reluctant to make this commitment.

- Access to PCs may not be universal; this is quite common in manufacturing and retailing environments where employees may access a common PC by means of a shared 'kiosk'.

- Cultural issues may inhibit the acceptance of self-service usage.

As the HR BP articulates their requirements for new applications it will be important to consider how elements like self-service and workflow technologies can best be deployed in the organization. They offer tangible benefits and yet may be constrained by technical, organizational or cultural issues that suggest they are not appropriate.

CHAPTER 8

Integrated Solutions or 'Best of Breed'

Close involvement with an HR technology project will demand that the HR BP develop a familiarity with some of the related concepts that determine the shape of the solution; for example, the strategy that the organization will adopt when buying and integrating HR applications.

There is a continuous debate in IT circles as to whether technology needs are best served by a single integrated solution from a single supplier covering a broad range of functionality or from a range of specialist stand-alone solutions sitting on top of a common database of people data (for example Web-based recruitment, learning management, performance management) which is sometimes referred to as a 'tools-on-top' or 'best-of-breed' strategy.

A dedicated learning management solution from a specialist supplier may provide more comprehensive functionality than an integrated system. However, one of the most significant challenges in adopting a multiple product approach to technology is in ensuring that the component parts of the solution work effectively together.

Any two applications that are not explicitly designed to share data and work in an integrated manner will require some form of bespoke interface. Many organizations have found that their 'best of breed' strategy, does not deliver the promised vision of best available functionality because of failings in this area.

These interfaces are often highly complex and expensive to build and they may create a potential point of failure in the system. Organizations that have pursued this route have often found that the advantage of superior functionality is quickly wiped out by a system with unreliable interfaces that does not adequately support the end-to-end process and relies on data held in different locations.

This does not mean that an HR systems strategy should not consider best-of-breed solutions where they provide genuine advantage. However, in a range of organizations surveyed by Orion Partners in 2003–04, poor integration was frequently cited as a major cause of systems failure.

As a general rule, organizations are advised to adopt a single integrated solution, probably from a single supplier, as a starting point. Any additional solutions or systems should be carefully evaluated in terms of the benefits they offer versus the cost and complexity they create.

An important message for anyone reviewing their HR systems strategy at this stage is that the variety and complexity of solutions available on the market currently will deliver most of the requirements that the Business Partner could want. However, at all stages in the process there will be other considerations that mean some trade-off of functionality may be required to reduce overall risk and complexity.

DECIDING WHAT YOU NEED

Bold objects require conservative engineering

James E. Webb

Business applications for HR carry a high degree of functionality, are generally available to all and they are easy to acquire. These qualities are both strengths and weaknesses. The advantages of technology solutions are open to all, but it is easy to create an illusion of progress by going out and buying software without truly understanding how the application will be used by the business. Furthermore, the complexity of a solution of this nature means it can easily become an end in itself and the business context in which it operates is forgotten. Some upfront investment of time in the development of a technology strategy for HR will provide much greater rigour to the project. We have frequently encountered projects that have lost sight of their original purpose and have become watered down to the point where they no longer deliver any benefit to the organization. Illustrating the case for investment will greatly reduce the likelihood that the solution may be arbitrarily scaled down to fit a budget later in the project.

A typical starting point would be to form an initial project team to drive the programme through the early stages of requirements definition, business case planning and solution selection. This team may go on to form part of the core team that undertakes out the development and implementation project that follows.

The members of the team at this stage of the process will have a critical impact on the quality of the final solution. IT representation is usually a given factor on technology projects of this nature and, by default, the project may become an IT-led process. Representation from HR, finance and, potentially, the businesses may be sought as the project progresses, but there is a great danger that the real strategic business issues will not be adequately addressed if this representation is too junior or too far removed from strategic planning in the HR function. Too many organizations have discovered too late that they have delivered projects that rated as technical successes without really making any qualitative change in the HR service itself.

In our view it is critical that the interests of the HR BP are represented early on in the project to ensure that the complexity of their clients' needs are fully represented and that critical management information will be available to support their role. Too often HR involvement is provided by the nearest available person. By definition a senior HR BP will be so valuable that releasing them to the project will be difficult, but this is precisely why their close involvement is so important.

In this chapter we will consider how this group might go about formulating a strategy for developing an HR solution and what principles should be applied to the governance of the solutions.

WHERE DOES IT HURT?

A good starting point for an HRIS strategy is an assessment of the current state of affairs. Whilst some new or growing organizations may be investing in technology for the first time, many will be addressing the need to replace dated or ineffective systems. We have already highlighted some of the common complaints surrounding dated or inadequate systems. An initial review of technology failings is likely to reveal a range of issues that constrain the HR function in different ways, as show in Figure 8.1.

Operational issues *'It stops us working'*	Tactical issues *'It stops us managing'*	Strategic issues *'It stops us changing'*
• Data are not complete • Data are inaccurate • We lack basic information • We are drowning in paper • Data sit in several places • System requires a lot of manual intervention • People aren't getting paid accurately and on time	• The system does not cover everyone • Only a few people can access data • Lack of qualitative data in critical areas – e.g. skills • We have no reporting tools • Data on different systems do not agree	• There is no end-to-end process • System drives the process not the other way around • No flexibility to change process • System will not support a new organizational model for HR • No universal access to PCs – dated IT architecture • We cannot forecast trends – we only know what happened in the past

Figure 8.1 Typical HR technology issues that constrain the HR function

TYPICAL ISSUES REDUCING THE IMPACT OF TECHNOLOGY ON THE HR FUNCTION

For the HR BP, key considerations at this stage will be how these types of issues impact their clients within the business and how the HR solution will have the potential to help them.

The lack of critical qualitative data is likely to be a key issue for senior managers and a key consideration for the Business Partner when defining their toolkit requirements.

Access to 'key people indicators' relating to pay, benefits and performance are likely to be high on the shopping list for the Business Partner's clients. However, good management information will be irrelevant if HR cannot underpin this with robust core processes relating to pay, resourcing and development, particularly if they are a core element of senior management strategy. Failure to deliver in these areas either now or in the future is always going to be a major barrier to the Business Partner's credibility with their client group.

WHERE ARE WE HEADING?

If stakeholders are polled at all levels of the organization, a pattern will emerge of the major shortcomings of the current systems. This information will provide valuable data to fuel the case for change and to inform the priorities of system delivery.

However, to provide genuine direction the strategy must also focus on how new systems will support key business objectives. The linkage between business strategy, HR strategy and technology strategy forms the most critical foundation for a successful system.

HR operations do not normally have generic technology requirements. The functional scope requirements of an HR system are influenced by the market sector and are further affected by a range of external factors which alter the demands on people processes and the need for HR data.

THE BUSINESS CONTEXT WILL HEAVILY INFLUENCE THE SYSTEMS REQUIREMENTS

The main objective for the HR BP is to pin down those technology factors that will have the biggest impact in terms of supporting their client businesses and HR objectives, and addressing the operational needs of the function (see Figure 8.2). Ultimately,

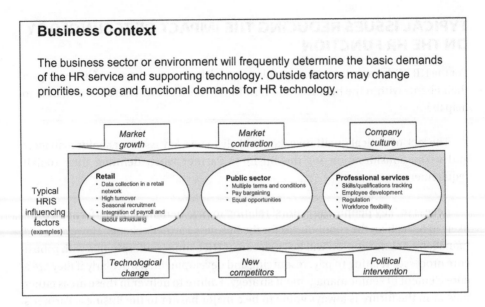

Figure 8.2   The external business context may change the scope and demands made of HR technology

fulfilling this objective will ensure that the system developed is rigorously linked to the requirements of the business and that the delivered functionality is prioritized according to the benefit it delivers rather than on the basis of 'nice to have' features.

There is no magic formula for making this determination. A good understanding of the organization and its priorities together with good knowledge of the available technology options will be key. The resulting analysis will typically highlight the main components of the HR plan that drive a technology requirement.

HR STRATEGY AND IMPLICATIONS FOR HR SYSTEMS

Clearly Figure 8.3 represents only an example of how the components of business and HR strategy may combine to drive technology requirements. The HR BP should start to develop an awareness of this linkage and, in particular, how their role is affected.

The Business Partner's need for access to accurate and timely HR data is in turn dependent on the integrity of the underlying HR process and the effectiveness of the technology that supports it. Any solution that does not address the need for robust core processes or closely integrated people systems is unlikely to produce meaningful management data. Unfortunately, this failure may only come to light in the later stages of the project, so a good understanding of this relationship at this early stage is vital.

The HR strategy takes its cue from the business imperatives of the organization; similarly the HR technology strategy must be able to demonstrate a clear linkage between the HR strategy and the component parts of the proposed system. Set out below is a real example produced for a client organization to demonstrate how key elements of the HR strategy drive technology requirements.

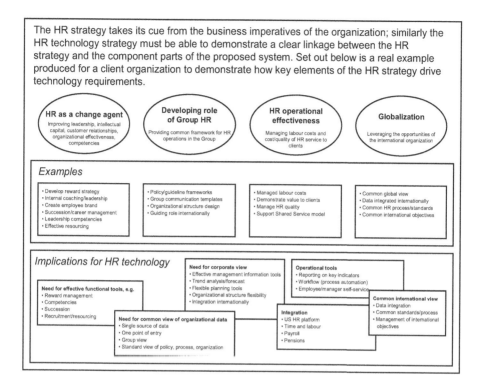

Figure 8.3 HR strategy and implications for HR systems

AGREEING SOME KEY PRINCIPLES

At this stage of the process the project team, and particularly the Business Partner, should consider some of the other key principles that will have direct bearing on how effectively the system will support the objectives of the business and the role of the Business Partner.

A full discussion of all factors for consideration in the course of a project of this nature would vastly increase the scope of this chapter and cover areas outside the remit of the HR BP. However, a useful checklist developed by Orion Partners covers the following areas as part of the HR technology strategy:

USER SCOPE

As we have discussed, the development of new systems alongside the delivery of new HR service models will introduce new roles and new requirements for access to HR data (core HR users, call centre staff, Business Partners, subject matter experts, line managers, employees). Each group of users will have a unique set of responsibilities within the HR process and, accordingly, will have different demands of the system. Whilst Figure 8.4 may serve as an outline view of the demands of various users, it will be important as part of the process of business requirements analysis to determine any further gradations of requirement within this model. For example, the concept of management information may be further refined into tools for historical reporting and tools of analysis that are capable of analysing trends. Whilst the former will be of interest to most people with HR management responsibility, the need to monitor and forecast trends in key performance data is a specialist requirement that is likely to be of interest to senior executives in the organization only.

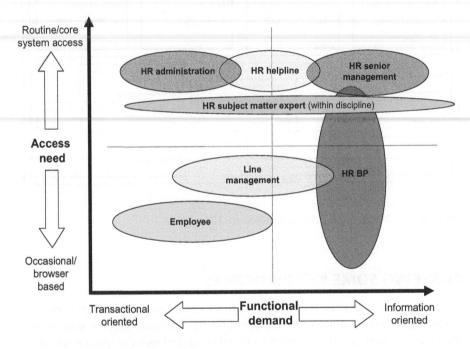

Figure 8.4   User demand by role

At the same time it is important to determine where scope may be cut back to reduce risk and complexity in the delivered solution. For example, the potential of manager self-service to enhance the range of functionality and information available to employees and managers is very high. However, an uncontrolled roll-out of self-service functionality to line managers is likely to result in a solution that is complex and difficult to maintain and where the cost of roll-out is likely to exceed the expected benefit.

Gaining an understanding of the potential user base, their requirements and constraints and the scope of their interest in HR systems, is an essential step in the development of an HR strategy to guide and inform the development process. Whilst subsequent stages of the project may re-address the issue of scope it is important to develop an initial view of key stakeholders who will use the system to ensure that there are no gaps in the requirement.

ACCESS AND SECURITY

As discussed above, different HR audiences will have differing demands of the system in terms of the functionality they require, but also the type of access they need. Figure 8.4 illustrates how the roles of HR users in the organization are likely to impact the type of access and functional requirements they have.

Many applications will support access either directly to the system by means of internal networks or via some form of web browser. One of the key considerations in early stage planning for HR systems is how the roles of different types of users will affect their requirements for access to different functionality and data; who will have entitlement to update the various forms of data is another key consideration.

Deciding on access and security requirements inevitably involves a careful balancing act to ensure that adequate controls and data protection compliance are in place, but at the same time system performance is not compromised by over-elaborate security requirements. Some level of compromise is likely to be required here and the Business Partner should understand the impact of the demands they are making on the system when determining access rights.

SCOPE OF HISTORICAL DATA

Determining the amount of historical data to import to the new system is also a matter for some debate. On the one hand, many payroll-related processes require access to historical data to support year-end processing. Similarly, many HR processes rely on access to a rich source of historical data to provide high-quality management information. Many might question the suggestion that some or even all historic data on existing systems are not carried forward to the new system.

However, as always, there are several counter-considerations to take into account. First, the current systems are being replaced for a reason: it is quite likely that the data they hold is incomplete or carries inaccuracies that have given rise to poor-quality management information.

Second, the scope of current systems may not be comprehensive. Legacy systems often fail to catch up with organizational changes such as mergers and acquisitions and may not carry data on all employees in the organization. Where data are held in the old system may reflect arbitrary differences between different parts of the organization so that, for example, grading structures, job definitions and organization structures are not held in the same way and cannot be reconciled readily between different parts of the business.

Last, new systems will probably represent a broader scope of functionality and it is quite likely that new data will need to be collected from scratch as new functionality is introduced.

Inevitably, it is only worth migrating data to the new system if the issues relating to accuracy, completeness and collection can be addressed. The process of cleaning up data prior to migrating it to a new system can be highly complex and time consuming (often reflecting the largest single expenditure of effort on the project). As many project managers will testify from experience, migration of historic data should only be carried out where there is a clear business need or business benefit to do so.

STANDARDIZATION

One of the most common issues relating to the replacement of HR systems is that different parts of the organization may have developed their own ways of managing core HR processes.

Different organizational and geographical units may have developed different approaches to recruitment, performance management and reward management. These reflect genuine business or local legislative needs or they may have evolved simply because units have been left to their own devices and their own way of doing things. Whatever the reason, any ambition to produce meaningful data at the group or organization-wide level will inevitably be frustrated if there is no common definition of a senior manager, a working week or a full-time employee.

Tackling the harmonization of process and data standards across the organization can be a painful and politically fraught process that requires careful consideration of the change management issues as HR working practices and procedures are brought into line. Business, regional and national differences may surface to present obstacles to the process; collective bargaining agreements may hinder new working arrangements and general resistance to change may make the process seem interminable.

Unsurprisingly, many organizations have elected to implement new systems using current data standards and processes vowing to return to the process issue once the new system is 'up and running'. Inevitably the new system fails to ever reach this happy state as development costs to meet multiple sets of requirements spiral, the benefits of improved management information fail to materialize and the new system begins to look suspiciously like the old system but with a more expensive cost base.

None of this means that the organization should adopt a 'one size fits all approach' to HR processes. Many organizations have failed to appreciate the cultural and legal implications of rolling out a standard approach in different geographical regions. The HR BP will have an important role in helping the organization define which parts of the process represent a unique requirement to their business and which can be accommodated within the group model.

Process and data standardization is one of the key success factors in any HR system delivery. This may be forced by the need to implement Shared Service arrangements in HR or it may need to be addressed independently in the HR systems project. Whichever approach is taken, the HR BP involved in the process of defining and delivering HR information systems must be prepared to get involved early in the horse trading that will determine how their business's process can be incorporated into a new common model.

GOVERNANCE

Who is to own and manage the delivered system may seem like a strange consideration during the early stages of the project. However, as discussed, many organizations will approach a project of this nature from a position of maintaining a wide range of disparate and disconnected applications for people data.

Poor systems create an environment where frustrated users are quite likely to build their own spreadsheets, local databases and, if they have the budget, local proprietary systems. Whilst understandable, this exacerbates the problem of 'the disconnected HR function' as people data become progressively distributed around the organization, resulting in little hope of meaningful aggregate data ever being produced.

A good governance structure, developed and communicated early and given sufficient senior sponsorship, will help ensure the integrity of the new system and reduce resistance from individuals who may be reluctant to surrender their pet systems. However, this is not to say that a common approach to HR systems based on a single supplier is always ideal from a group perspective. Many corporations have faced the issue of different operating divisions or regions with conflicting technology strategies or long-standing investment in different application platforms.

Rather than forcing a company line, many organizations have taken the view that their business units are free to pursue their own strategy provided they can support corporate requirements for common people data aggregated in a particular way. For example, corporate strategy may dictate a common process and software application for a global process, such as resourcing top-tier professionals. This may be coupled with a common set of reporting standards for this data but would not preclude local HR functions from adding to the corporate specification to meet their own needs.

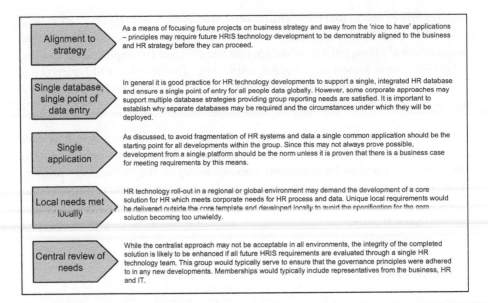

Figure 8.5 HR system governance principles: examples

Early consideration of the replacement of particular legacy applications in the business is essential if last-minute reworking of development and roll-out plans is to be avoided. The principal HR system governance principles that should be followed are summarized in Figure 8.5.

Adherence to these principles will ensure that HRIS programmes are well managed and that the chances of successful implementation are significantly enhanced.

CHAPTER 9

Functional Scope and Business Requirements

The full functional scope will be largely determined by the scope of activities defined within the HR strategy. However, a high-level review of market offerings will often demonstrate the 'art of the possible' and use of a simple taxonomy for HR will highlight any potential gaps in the requirement (see Figure 9.1).

Figure 9.1 A summary of the core activities in-scope for HRIS projects

The functional scope that is outlined as part of the HR strategy will eventually form the basis for a more comprehensive document that details the full functional and technical requirements.

Such analyses as those leading to this document are generally required to support key stages of the project including the selection, design and development of systems and most IT functions will determine the standard forms and content of the document. Typical contents for a full functional and technical requirements document would include the following:

- *Background and context*: A summary of the business context of the project and the main business drivers for the project should be developed which is sufficient to give third-party providers of software and services an understanding of the critical business issues. This will place them in a position to recommend the best approaches.

- *Options for delivery:* The consideration of any options for the scope, phasing or approach to the project is needed. High-priority requirements that should be tackled first in the project or critical dependencies that will affect the project, such as the timing and availability of critical hardware infrastructure, are examples of options.

- *Functional requirements*: Detailed business definitions of the main functional areas and the process and data requirements of the system should be given. This information should be sufficient to determine how the process will work and identify any unique or business-specific issues that need to be addressed. At the same time it is important to recognize that a detailed systems design will be carried out later in the process and is probably not required here.

- *Architecture requirements:* Assumptions or dependencies relating to the delivery of the new system should be examined. They may include, for example, assumptions relating to the availability of PCs for all staff that will use self-service environments and, similarly, the availability of a network with sufficient bandwidth to cope with this requirement in all locations.

- *Interfaces:* A description of the major interfaces or exchange of information between the HR system and other applications is needed. The extent of the definition will depend on the nature of the interface. Complex interfaces such as those between HR and payroll may require definition of the main data items to be transferred between each system, as well as the timing of such events, any validation that is carried out by each system before it is accepted and how exceptions to the process are to be managed. Clearly, if HR and payroll systems are sourced from a single supplier offering an integrated solution then much of this will be delivered in the integrated product. Less complete interfaces, for example those involving only a one-way flow of data, will still require some definition in terms of the type and frequency of data passed.

- *Volumes:* An overview of the type and volume of transactions and data the system will be required to manage should be included. This provides essential information for sizing and costing both hardware and software solutions and is likely to include annual figures for:

  - employee numbers (monthly, weekly and four-weekly paid)
  - numbers of leavers held on the systems
  - applicants, new recruits, leavers and transfers
  - record changes
  - absences
  - user numbers by category of user.

MANAGEMENT INFORMATION

Effective management information is probably the single most important requirement for the Business Partner when considering their HR information needs. Their relationship with the business will be based on the provision of:

- an effective and efficient operational service;
- a clear understanding and articulation of current status in the business;
- proactivity in the business to support future direction.

The key to providing a high-quality response to the last two points lies in access to high-quality management information and probably reflects one of the key reasons for investing in the new system. Indeed, the lack of basic management information in HR is frequently cited as one of the major frustrations (for example, 'We can't even get a basic headcount') and systems that do not deliver in this area will rapidly lose credibility with the business. However, despite management information's importance, it is often not considered in detail as an independent requirement.

Management information is frequently considered to be a by-product of good administrative procedures and this is correct to an extent. An effective recruitment process will compile data about an applicant at each stage of the process, building to a complete profile as they become a new employee. If the process is managed via a recruitment system, then the system will also probably capture management information regarding recruitment cycle times, acceptance/rejection rates and equal opportunities: all potential performance indicators in the recruitment process.

However, whilst this is fine in theory, unless a number of key system design factors have been considered, extracting management information in a usable format will not be straightforward and the system may fail to deliver the expected management information benefits. In this chapter we will explore the different types of management information, who uses them and what are the key demands on the system; we will also look at the main considerations during design that will impact the successful production of management information.

TYPES OF MANAGEMENT INFORMATION

A useful starting point is considering the types of information which may be defined as management information. Its users may range from senior executives to relatively junior staff making operational decisions, and its formats may vary from complex standard reports incorporating data from multiple sources to simple queries which may be output to a computer screen. For our purposes we have broken this down into three basic types:

- *Operational management information:* The day-to-day requirements for information to support ongoing operational processes are known as operational management information. This may include queries to which clients in the business may expect rapid answers or wish to retrieve themselves ('How many people in X?', 'What is the average turnover in Y?' and so on). Failure on the part of the HR BP to answer these most basic of queries accurately and promptly will lead to an immediate loss of credibility for both the Business Partner and the system. Key criteria for this type of management information include query tools that are simple to use, rapid access to appropriate systems and data ('I need it now!') and the flexibility to respond to unpredictable questions.

- *Tactical management information:* If operational management information relates to day-to-day operations, tactical management information is about monitoring and analysing the progress and performance of HR operations. Examples include the measurement of key performance indicators in HR, routine workforce statistics, standard payroll outputs and any area where aggregated data is required to measure some aspect of business performance. Once again, the Business Partner is likely to be required to produce these data or make them accessible to their clients. Whilst this information may not be required instantly it is likely to be needed consistently, in other words to regular schedules, with consistent formats and definitions and formatted to the requirements of the recipients. The flexibility to extract data with different analyses, format outputs and schedule outputs to be produced automatically are likely to be key.

- *Strategic management information:* Many organizations claim the need for strategic data as being their primary driver for investment in new systems.

However, interestingly, there appears to be no common view of what constitutes strategic management information in the HR function. If the organization is starting from a baseline of having no management information, then the ability to produce some fairly basic statistics can feel quite strategic. Software suppliers have responded with a range of tools that fall into the 'analytics' category. These differ from standard reporting tools in that they incorporate progress against business objectives into their answers to inform senior management when they are meeting or missing their projected targets. Such analytics tools can be highly effective when coupled with a balanced scorecard approach that consistently monitors a range of performance indicators and spots trends that may lie outside the parameters set by strategic plans. Problem areas or hotspots can be highlighted to executives by means of simple traffic-light mechanisms (red for 'Off-target and requires management action', amber for 'Requires close tracking as slippage is occurring' and green for 'OK, proceeding to plan') so that executive time can be spent here and not on areas that are working effectively.

Such tools may appear as part of an 'expert analytics' package that provides monitoring and forecasting capability to subject-matter experts about their functions. At more senior levels 'executive analytics' may marry data from a wide range of sources including HR, finance and customer management solutions to focus on business-wide issues.

To produce this type of information requires a significant degree of integration across multiple applications and is increasingly the objective behind integrated, single-supplier approaches to business applications.

All of the software vendors we spoke to cited the growth of interest in human capital asset reporting as a major driver behind their investment in these technologies. A common message was that senior executives are less interested in 'HR data' *per se* and are more interested in how they can be combined with other data assets in the organization to answer directional questions for the business.

The purpose of such tools may be summarized as an attempt to standardize the non-standard. Whilst managers may take pride in their organizational capabilities, at the most senior levels there is frequently a requirement to display powers of disorganization – that is, the ability to ask difficult and disruptive questions about the status quo. At this level the functional distinctions of HR, finance and customer data disappear; the Business Partner's job is to ensure that their data are closely aligned and integrated with other forms of data in the organization.

Garbage in, garbage out?

- *Data standards:* The phrase 'We can't even produce a simple headcount' is regularly repeated in organizations lacking basic HR systems. Whilst this requirement may appear laughably simple, the request is often not as straightforward as it sounds. Accurate headcount is dependent on a agreement in a number of areas:

  - agreeing at what point in time the headcount is taken (headcount may change daily);
  - agreeing who is an employee (do you count contractors or staff on maternity leave or sabbatical?);
  - agreeing what you are counting (do you count heads or full-time equivalents; how do you count part-timers?).

  Without agreeing these criteria any two headcounts will not agree (and yet may be perfectly accurate). What this illustrates is the need, on a corporate level, to agree reporting and data standards so that critical management information does agree.

  Reporting across geographical or organizational lines may require those parts of the organization to agree on basic definitions like 'full-time', 'grade', 'total salary' and 'good performance'. These definitions are an essential prerequisite for the production of corporate data but may be constrained where different organizational or geographical units have pursued independent approaches to HR. To achieve the required levels of corporate management information it may be necessary to effect a change in the definition of common HR data items in different parts of the business.

- *Data cleansing:* The poor quality and unreliability of data on existing HR systems are often a primary reason to move systems. Inevitably implementation requires some consideration of the quality of existing data, how they will be cleaned up and how new data not previously held will be collected and entered on the new system. Many implementation processes require some form of contact with all current employees to check and collect these data. This can be a time-consuming and difficult task but it is important that the Business Partner is rigorous in their demands relating to the quality of data.

- *Organization structures:* As previously discussed, organizations may need to consider, for the first time, whether they wish to make investment in maintaining an organization hierarchy to support self-service functionality in HR. However, HR is not the only function that may use self-service and it is not uncommon to find that finance or customer management systems also drive self-service from the organizational structure.

A problem may arise if the organizational structure does not represent the HR view of the organization but is related to, say, a cost code structure. HR will need to ensure that the data on the system can be extracted in a way that is meaningful. For example, there is no point in extracting departmental appraisal data by cost centre if a particular department cannot be isolated in this way.

CHAPTER 10

The Business Case for Technology Investment

THE PURPOSE OF THE BUSINESS CASE

In all the projects we looked at in researching this book, the business case was the one area where there was most divergence in terms of approach, the level of detail included and the rigour with which the cost/benefits case was made.

In many ways the key arguments for the value of technology investment in HR are similar to the case for investment in the HR function itself. For organizations that take a view of the HR function as an overhead to the organization, the arguments for technology tend to be focused on reducing that overhead – 'How can we reduce HR headcount and other operating costs?' – which inevitably leads to 'How can we do this project for less money?' Ultimately, this technology case serves to further reduce the strategic value of HR and a vicious circle of cost reduction and, frequently, service reduction is created.

However, for organizations that value the strategic contribution of the HR function and seek to drive increased performance and competitive behaviour through the use of best-practice people policies, the case for technology may be centred on service enhancement and competitive advantage. The role of technology in this model, whilst often difficult to cost, is considered an essential part of the Business Partner's toolkit.

What is clear is that, without serious consideration of the potential benefits of technology and the case for investment, HR will rarely contribute to the step changes in performance seen in organizations with a best-practice approach to HR.

Whilst it is possible to drive out operational savings through process and organizational redesign, ultimately the next level of benefit will derive from revised models of HR service. All of these changes carry heavy demands in terms of integrated processes to support the smooth running of lean operations and management information to support business and subject-matter specialists working in the capacity of advisers to the business. These changes will not come from the kind of legacy systems that are fragmented, poorly maintained and lack HR-specific functionality.

The main purpose of the business case is to set the agenda for the proposed change in HR technology and to identify the component costs and the benefits that the organization may expect as a result. The business case may be made in the context of other proposed changes (for example plans to move to a Shared Service Centre environment) and may therefore be considered an enabler of the delivery of new service models.

Generally, the business case will be used to drive a decision at senior levels on whether the proposed expenditure on HR technology is justified and whether the project can proceed. Too often, however, once project approval is gained, the business case is consigned to a drawer whilst the team get on with the serious business of delivering the system. This approach is a recipe for disaster. It ensures that the delivered system becomes disconnected from the promises made in the benefits case. In this chapter, therefore, we will examine the ways in which organizations tackle this issue and look at benefits tracking and benefits focused planning for projects.

The main headings we will consider in relation to the business case are as follows:

- use of third parties to support the business case
- preparing the cost model
- the benefits case
- selling the case to the board.

THE USE OF THIRD PARTIES TO SUPPORT THE BUSINESS CASE

The initiation of the business case discussion is frequently the first point at which the organization will engage with outside parties in relation to the project.

The need to identify sound cost estimates will involve obtaining quotes on software licences, technology architecture and implementation services from suppliers. Considerations of long-term support for the application may require an examination of the application and architecture outsource market. Similarly, if the new service-delivery model for HR is dependent on an outsourced business process model then these suppliers and their technology offerings may also be factored into the equation.

Anyone who has engaged in this type of analysis before will be painfully aware of the sales machines that each of these organizations employs and which are likely to develop a significant interest in the technology project now that the serious business of obtaining funding is at hand.

In fairness, most suppliers of technology services will engage account teams at senior levels in the organization and make a substantial year-round investment in understanding the business context of new projects so that they are well positioned to support this type of initiative. However, for the project manager driving the business case, the sudden arrival of account teams and sales consultants, all anxious to understand the project background and push the merits of their own solutions, can be seen as an unwelcome distraction from the main task.

It is important to realize that, as the requirement for HR information and process support is explored in more detail, so the complexity of the required solution may also grow. The task of pushing self-service applications out to remote locations in order to facilitate organizational change in HR may demand a consideration of the business's requirements for new software, hardware and network infrastructures as well as hosting and support. It is highly unlikely that a project team working solely with internal resources will be able to scope and cost such a solution accurately for the business case. Engagement with the relevant sales teams to understand their offerings, costs and dependencies will be crucial.

For those not experienced in dealing with professional sales teams the temptation may be to keep them as much as possible at arms' length, approaching them only when you require information and giving away as little as possible in the interim. In general, however, sales people will respond well to someone who is a consistent and reliable source of information about the project. An honest appraisal of the business need, scope and likelihood of obtaining funding will enable sales teams to make a good early qualification of their likelihood of success and, hence, the level of effort they are prepared to make in supporting you. The more a sales team is able to look to you as a reliable source of information, the less likely they are to chase that information in other parts of the organization.

Once on-side, third-party suppliers can provide an invaluable source of information to support the planning and business case process. As well as giving information on costs and available discounts they will frequently be able to provide examples of how other organizations have tackled similar issues and the type of benefits they were able to realize. Many suppliers have taken a leaf from the consulting markets and have introduced their own return on investment models or other tools to demonstrate the benefits of their solutions.

Such 'qualified benefits' will form an important part of the process of selling the project internally at Board level. Clearly, however, all sales teams are engaged in the business of selling their product and the project manager cannot rely wholly on their advice to define the project. For this reason, many organizations seek the support of specialist consulting firms to advise on the planning, design, business case and implementation process.

At this point many beleaguered project managers will point out that such consultants simply represent another supplier relationship in the process that has to be equally carefully managed and, of course, they are correct. As a provider of technology consulting services we maintain our own sales process and client relationships; however, our own differentiator is that we provide advice that is independent of the solution that is chosen. This is an important distinction for a number of reasons.

The phenomenal growth of the systems integration consulting market in recent years has created some unholy alliances. Consultant organizations that previously declared their independence in the process, now depend heavily on the consultancy business derived from the implementation of the two major ERP suppliers (Oracle/PeopleSoft and SAP). To deliver complex systems integration projects, many consultancies maintain teams of consultants dedicated to a particular solution and their own sales teams will often work in close alliance with those of the software supplier.

A business may therefore have no idea that a particular consultancy is working closely with the software supplier who recommended them or vice versa. The joint targeting of 'key accounts' by technology suppliers and consultancies may be invisible to the businesses that buy their services, so the meaning of 'independent adviser' should be closely examined.

A truly independent adviser should not receive payment from a supplier or be reliant on that supplier for a major part of their business; these factors are often not disclosed when 'independent advice' is offered. A truly independent adviser should be able to provide clear guidance and opinions on the way forward. A consultant who will not come off the fence is of little use to the project team, who need clear answers as to the relative strengths and weaknesses of the solutions offered. We will consider later how this works in relation to vendor selection.

PREPARING THE COST MODEL

Pinning down the component parts of the costs of a solution can be a complex and frustrating task.

On the one hand, suppliers, whilst keen to push the advantages of their products, may be reluctant to present costs for a wide range of modules for fear of sinking the business case. Consequently the project manager will need to develop a detailed understanding of what the supplier offers and precisely what is needed to meet their business's requirements.

On the other hand, an internal team may take the view that costs should be presented as conservatively as possible. Building up a cost profile on a 'worst case scenario' basis can frequently make the project seem unviable before it gets off the ground. Indeed, we have seen several projects where the initial estimate of costs exceeds the final estimate by a factor of three or more.

Clearly a middle way is required that provides a thorough and honest appraisal of solution costs whilst ensuring that the principal variables affecting costs have been pinned down as far as possible.

As discussed in the above, the cost information may well be derived from several sources and the responsibility will be on the project manager to ensure that a full analysis of costs has been completed.

COST COMPONENTS

Software licence

Software providers typically sell licences to organizations wishing to use the different modules of their software. Additional costs may be incurred for the use of the supplier's underlying database products and management information tools.

An overview of the typical component modules in an HR application is provided above. Project managers must ascertain which modules support the scope of functionality they require and cost them accordingly. A key consideration will be the levels of discount that a software supplier may be prepared to allow on their products which in turn will be influenced by the range and volume of products being purchased and any existing relationships they may have and product usage there may be within the organization or group.

Care should be taken with any quotes obtained from suppliers as part of a 'bundled' deal; particularly if the organization subsequently decides to reduce the scope of the project and procure fewer modules as this will inevitably lead the supplier to reconsider their costs. Consideration should also be given to when the organization would wish to incur a cost. A supplier is likely to discount on the basis that all quoted modules are purchased at the same time, whereas an organization with a project that runs for 18 months or more may not wish to acquire modules that they will not deploy for over a year.

Last, on the subject of software licences: consideration should be given to additional third-party licences that may be required to work in support of the new application. Whilst the range of possible software applications is enormous, the list might include software to support third-party reporting, case management for the call centre environment and knowledge repository software to manage information on staffing policy to support helpline services.

Technical architecture

The design and configuration of large-scale networks and support infrastructure are specialized skills in their own right and will not be explored in detail here. However, the project manager should be mindful of the importance of reviewing the technical architecture needs for the new solution.

Self-service applications may create significant demands for more bandwidth in the network to support on-line business transactions. New applications may require additional servers to manage data, access to Web environments and the application itself. The availability of applications to third parties, for example allowing recruitment agencies to access e-recruitment applications, may create demands for firewalls and additional security for current systems.

The impact of the requirements for new technical architecture is easy to underestimate and so they should be carefully evaluated in the business case by appropriate professionals.

Application development and delivery

This covers a wide range of activities associated with the delivery of the new solution and relates predominantly to people costs.

One of the most significant costs is around the use of third parties to support the delivery of the project. Clearly the extent to which third parties are used will depend on the availability of internal resources. For example, organizations implementing a wide range of products from a major ERP vendor may have internal access to technical skills in the product. However, the likelihood is that undertaking the implementation of a major ERP application suite will require support in one of several areas:

- application design (establishing how the application will need to be configured to meet the needs of the business)
- development (configuring and customizing the core application to meet the design criteria)
- testing
- data conversion
- training
- deployment of the system in separate geographical locations.

In addition, related activities including the design, development and deployment of related technology architecture should be considered. Depending on the state of the current IT infrastructure, this may be a relatively straightforward task or it may require major investment and delivery activity to meet the needs of the new application. Such a situation may not be uncommon, for example, where the HR application is the first major application in the organization to deploy self-service functionality. This, in turn, may necessitate investment in additional network bandwidth to cope with the additional transactional activity.

On the business side of the equation, the systems delivery project may have to synchronize with the development of new process and organizational models for HR. The application design activities, for example, may have to take their lead from the process of defining HR processes in a service centre oriented environment; this may involve the HR Business Partners, HR process expertise and application experts.

In identifying costs for project resources, consideration needs to be given as to where they will be sourced. Internal resources may be expected to carry a low or zero cost and this may be true, for example, of HR resources seconded on to a project from the HR team. However, IT resources are often costed as an internal consultancy service and, in some circumstances, may be as expensive as some external resources. Using internal teams is not a guarantee of low cost!

In situations where IT services are outsourced, the project manager may have no choice but to cost resources from the incumbent services supplier and may find that costs for deploying or supporting the IT infrastructure are non-negotiable.

This dependency on the outsourcer is frequently compounded by the lack of availability of internal resources to support such a specialist task as the deployment of the application. Even if the organization does have staff with the requisite skills, the turnover amongst these staff is notoriously high.

It is likely that the project manager will need to consider using specialist application skills from outside the organization. There are many sources of such skills; all of the major consulting firms maintain specialist teams skilled in the main application sets. These firms specialize in the deployment of complete solutions and will typically offer services that represent a 'one-stop shop' in terms of access to business process, application development and technical skills as part of the same team. However, whilst consultancy markets have taken a significant downturn in recent years, the costs of such 'total solution' offerings are usually high by comparison with some of the other options.

A variety of niche players have developed to service specialist markets and it is not difficult to find small consulting firms that specialize in Oracle or SAP products; often such organizations will have expertise in particular applications and there are now several that service the HR market alone. Using a niche player may not dramatically reduce the costs of the project. Although the day rates for niche consultancies may start at a lower level than those of the major players, open competition for the business will often bring rates much closer in line. The most significant trade-off for the project manager will be the in-depth services and skills that a niche player can offer versus the capability of the larger players to leverage skills in related project areas and in different geographies.

A genuine reduction in day rate may be realized by resourcing the project directly using external contractors with the requisite skill sets. This approach can offer significant price advantages; however, the risk of having to manage a disparate team of individuals who may have never worked together before may more than offset this advantage. Many organizations have found to their cost that one of the main advantages of using a consultancy operation to manage a major project is the short cuts they can bring to the process as a result of having undertaken similar work. Such an advantage is lost if the project is resourced solely from the contract market.

A relatively recent dimension in the delivery service market is the emergence of options for offshore delivery. The use of offshore firms in places like India, China and Eastern Europe to deliver deep technical skills at very low cost has been well tried and tested; the emergence of offshore players in the application delivery market is a newer phenomenon.

At first sight such a proposition may be unattractive for delivering a project that requires strong understanding of business process in HR, possibly coupled with local knowledge of the legislative framework, neither of which are natural territory for the offshore providers. However, the offshore market has responded to demand in this area by greatly improving their business expertise in supporting the application implementation business. The latest generation of offshore offerings has seen the traditional technical skills offered by the offshore providers coupled with the business process and legislative knowledge of local providers to provide genuine low-cost delivery services whilst reducing the risk of employing pure technical delivery services.

THE BENEFITS CASE

The approach to defining the benefits of investment in HR technology varies immensely. In some organizations the case for investment in HR and people-related systems is taken as read; the benefits case for HR systems is simply a matter of defining how the functions and information provided by the new system will work in support of the accepted HR strategy.

For most organizations, however, the task is significantly more difficult. One of the major problems is the perception of HR in the business as a whole. A historical view of HR as an administrative function that has added little value to the organization is not a strong precursor to large-scale systems investment, no matter that this may be the very issue that the planned changes are trying to address.

Consequently the task in selling the need for investment in HR technology is frequently an uphill struggle. The business case for HR technology will often need to demonstrate a much higher level of resilience than would a case for new financial or supply chain applications where the nature of such systems tends to be much closer to the core of the business and the belief, at senior levels, that 'this is a good thing to do', is much greater.

Fortunately, however, making the case for investment in HR technology is not as difficult as it might appear provided the case is tied effectively to other planned changes in the HR organization.

TYPES OF BENEFIT

HR system benefits usually fall into three categories and most business investment auditors will require some consideration of all levels. The three key types of benefit are discussed below.

Hard benefit

Hard benefit is strictly defined as tangible cash savings arising directly from the introduction of new technology. The definition of 'tangible' may vary in different organizations but the strictest interpretation would be to limit it to costs that currently reside in a clearly identifiable budget that may be reduced by a specified amount in coming years. As may be expected, there is a limited number of sources of such benefits but they typically fall into one of the following areas:

Headcount savings

Headcount savings can be made when staff numbers are reduced as a result of the new system. Typically this will comprise of savings arising from either isolated improvements in operational efficiency in HR or, on a larger scale, from the reorganization of the way in which HR services are delivered.

Whilst isolated improvements in current processes can be identified thanks to the new system (for example, the effort in preparing correspondence, entering data or preparing management information is reduced) these are likely to be limited if they are only viewed in the context of the organization in its present state.

More significant savings can be made if the full HR business process and the reorganization of HR are considered. For example, reorganization into an SSC or outsourced environment will typically provide a significant opportunity to streamline the end-to-end business process and group administrative services. This in turn offers the opportunity to realize headcount savings both in the HR function and in other parts of the business that may be carrying out 'invisible HR work' arising from a previous lack of service from HR. Whilst the precise level of saving may vary, a reduction of 25–30 per cent of HR headcount is not uncommon for organizations that have previously managed HR in a very devolved or inefficient manner. Clearly these savings are not simply related to the delivery of technology but need to be tied to the analysis and business case for the move to a new service delivery model.

Technology savings

The decommissioning of existing systems in HR is likely to generate some level of cost saving in its own right. Earlier in this chapter we highlighted the common complaints regarding legacy HR technology including the fragmentation of data and the development of isolated, stand-alone solutions to meet individual needs across the organization. An important consideration in the replacement of these systems is the current cost of ownership. Despite the fact that current systems may deliver little in terms of useful process support or management information, the costs of supporting and maintaining them can often be significant.

In particular, consideration should be given to the costs associated with current systems in the following related areas:

- software licence maintenance and support

- internal and contracted IT support costs

- hardware/server maintenance.

CASE STUDY: Retail

A retail organization with over 40 000 employees derived very little value from existing HR systems. Despite the existence of an integrated HR/payroll platform, analysis demonstrated this was predominantly focused on delivering the payroll process with very little effective HR management information being produced. Most available HR data resided on separate-access databases that involved a high level of manual manipulation.

Third-party products developed to collect data on HR and pay at store level were poorly integrated with core systems, resulting in an imperfect payroll process and frequent errors and inaccuracies.

> Initial findings revealed that the current fragmented architecture cost in excess of £1m annually to support – this was similar to the running costs of a fully integrated replacement solution. This figure coupled with the anticipated headcount savings arising from developing an SSC environment, suggested a total payback for technology investment of £4m in approximately two or three years. The organization is now formalizing these findings in a detailed business case.

Cost avoidance

Although much can be fabricated in terms of cost avoidance, as it can easily be argued that if Y is spent then X future cost will be avoided, this should really relate only to previously budgeted projects that can be abandoned (planned spend cancelled) as a result of the new investment. A typical example would be the planned upgrade or development of current platforms.

Upgrading to new releases of an existing application may be a contractual obligation for the organization. Similarly, investing in the development of legacy systems to meet changes in legislation, accommodating organizational changes or effecting significant changes in current process may all constitute projects which may be discarded as a result of the investment in new systems.

Reduction in third party costs

The use of third parties to support critical or high-volume activities is a regular feature of modern HR functions. As a result, HR has become a significant procurer of services relating to a range of functions such as recruitment, training, compensation and benefits management, payroll and pensions.

We have dealt elsewhere in this book with the strategic shift to outsourcing some or all components of HR as part of a shift in the way HR services are delivered. However, there is a distinction between this type of outsourcing and that which may have happened in a fragmented manner over time largely because the organization did not have the manpower or the systems to run the process effectively in-house.

Investing in new information systems in HR may afford several opportunities to reconsider these third-party relationships and the costs associated with them. Improvements in administrative processing and management data may afford HR the opportunity to reduce reliance on these third parties significantly or even dispense with them altogether, bringing some operations back in-house without a significant increase in workload or deterioration of the service.

For example, the extent and usage of recruitment agencies to recruit to vacancies is frequently fragmented or masked by a lack of available information. An integrated recruitment application may provide improved capability to track usage of agencies and manage the resourcing of vacancies in a more cost-effective manner. More importantly, the organization may develop the capability to record and track previous applications to the organization, thus creating its own vacancy pool and, in effect, becoming its own recruitment agency.

CASE STUDY: The tourism and leisure industry

A tourism and leisure operative was involved in high-volume seasonal recruitment (up to 40 per cent of the workforce). A lean recruitment operating model and the lack of available technology systems meant that service levels offered to prospective candidates were low. In addition, some elements of the initial sifting service were outsourced to a third-party provider at a relative high cost.

The business case for HR technology investment demonstrated an opportunity to improve service levels significantly through the automation of the production of correspondence to candidates. In addition, the use of third-party resource to support the candidate sifting process was reduced by 40 per cent in the first year.

Furthermore, the operative's ability to maintain a database of good potential applicants to support recruitment in the following season enabled them to reduce current advertising and recruitment budgets by a further 20 per cent.

In total, over £500 000 in annual savings were identified.

Opportunity benefit

Many of the benefits offered by an HR information system will relate to new opportunities to realize improvements in process or service. However, not all of these improvements will result in a direct cash saving of the sort identified above; some will create the opportunity to make new savings as a result of some additional action.

Two classic examples of such opportunity savings are in the areas of absence management and staff turnover. There is no doubt that uncontrolled staff absence and excessively high levels of staff turnover represent a significant cost and risk to the organization. HR systems can provide the infrastructure for monitoring patterns of absence and the root causes of staff turnover so that management action can be initiated to address them.

Part of the attraction of these benefits in relation to the business case is that they can very quickly generate large potential savings. Reducing staff absence by a percentage has a directly attributable benefit that can be quantified in terms of payroll costs. However, simply monitoring absence will not make someone turn up to work and making them turn up will not guarantee their performance when they get there. It cannot be said that the system provides a direct hard saving in this instance although it clearly plays a part in the process of addressing staff-related issues in the organization.

Clearly, other management initiatives are required on top of the HR system and a business case that relies on these types of savings alone is unlikely to receive approval at senior levels in the organization. Such arguments should be used in conjunction with the hard benefits identified at the previous stage, the organization is unlikely to be swayed by the need to invest in technology if the payback is solely dependent on some yet-to-be-defined course of management action.

Whilst the organization may or may not choose to recognize such savings as part of the overall business case for investment, we would argue that they are a critical part of the overall picture of the benefits of investment in HR technology. A balanced business case will demonstrate the strong potential offered by new technology to improve the quality of management in the organization and that there are wider benefits to be gained.

Service-level improvements

Whilst the business case analysis may have quantified some level of cash savings, there are many other ways in which the application of technology can improve the quality of HR service. Many of these benefits will be tied up in the case for new HR service delivery models. However, in general, improvements in HR technology can be said to have a positive impact in a number of HR service areas that will lend weight to the business case, including:

- improved data integrity/accuracy;

- faster response to queries – more accurate, better-informed decisions;

- faster response to requests for management information;

- more effective trend analysis and the potential to initiate proactive management;

- improved service levels to external candidates (faster response/better feedback);

- better focused and targeted training and learning initiatives;

- reducing risk by eliminating service failures and missed data entry due to glitches;

- alignment of HR service to business, providing the opportunity to create dedicated resource for generalist advice/centralization of operational tasks.

SELLING THE CASE TO THE BOARD

The consolidation of cost and benefit data into a formal financial appraisal of the proposed project is a task frequently undertaken by project appraisal specialists whose role may cover several areas:

- analysis of the completeness of costs

- validation/audit of proposed benefits

- calculation of organization-specific measures of business case value (for example internal rate of return, net present value of expenditure)

- recommendation to proceed.

Project appraisal methods vary immensely and there is no common agreed method for determining whether a project will proceed. Many regulated or public sector businesses will have intensely complex appraisal processes to determine the net value of HR systems investment. Frequently, such organizations will only consider the contribution of hard benefits towards offsetting the costs, regarding opportunity savings and service-level enhancements as immaterial to the business case.

Other organizations may take a far more relaxed view of what constitutes a valid investment case, relying to a far greater extent on developing an understanding of how the technology will transform the HR service model.

Clearly, neither approach is intrinsically correct and the one that is taken will depend on the organization's view of the value of technology investment, its economic position, current markets and, not least, the organization's attitude towards HR. Views of HR as either an administrative overhead to be reduced or as a critical strategic element in the overall business strategy will inevitably influence decisions on technology investment in HR and on the type of applications in which the organization is prepared to invest.

Any presentation of the case for approval should take account of all of these factors if it is to stand any chance of success. In particular, the Business Partner hoping to persuade the organization to invest in technology should consider the following questions when presenting the business case:

- Are the requirements clearly understood and do all parts of the business buy into them? Has the process of seeking compromise on current ways of working achieved a common agreed approach or have some parts of the organization been alienated?

- Are the costs comprehensive and realistic? Are all the major components of cost covered? Are internal as well as external costs considered? Have the costs been pressure tested with appropriate professionals in IT and HR as well as any external experts involved in the process?

- Are the benefits clearly articulated? Are the hard benefits genuine and auditable? Can they readily be identified as budgetary reductions? Are claims for improved service levels and opportunity savings supported by a revised model for HR service delivery?

- Has the appropriate level of financial appraisal been carried out? Have the right people been involved in the approval process? Have investment appraisal procedures been followed?

- Have the senior level stakeholders been brought along with the business case as it has developed or are they going to be hearing about this for the first time when a request for £Xm hits the boardroom table? Who around that table is going to support the proposition, who is neutral and who will oppose?

In conclusion, the HR BP will increasingly need to be technically savvy, understand the benefits that targeted investment in IT can bring, be able to work with specialist teams to implement and leverage technologies and be able to argue the case for investment in the platforms that allow new ways of working to be rolled out across both the staff and customers of HR. This chapter has only skimmed the surface of many issues but it has highlighted those clear areas where the effective Business Partner can, and is increasingly expected to, play a major role in the shaping and implementation of technology within an organization.

PART 3

Completing the Jigsaw

CHAPTER 11

The Role of the HR BP – The Line Manager's Viewpoint

This chapter looks at HR from the viewpoint of the business and draws conclusions from the line manager's perspective on why some HR BP initiatives succeed while many fail.

HR AND ITS REPUTATION

If you survey HR Directors about the reputation of their function in the business you get a telling response. First, it is clear that HR departments rarely ask the business 'How are we doing?'. Second, HR is, at best, perceived in a neutral way but more usually has a poor standing in the business. Surveys, when they are done, often elicit comments along the lines of 'I won't take HR seriously until they can start paying people correctly' or 'I got advice from HR on a disciplinary issue and now I've ended up with a tribunal on my hands'. Analysis often shows that HR is generally not at fault but these types of comments do reveal the mountain HR has to climb before it can be seen as a real partner to the business.

The HR function is a bit like a car engine. Most people never think about the inner workings of their car. They just leap in, put the key in the ignition and, day or night, rain or shine, they turn the key, start the engine and away they go. But when that engine doesn't fire at the first attempt, everyone hears about it. 'Don't buy an X car – they are really unreliable'; 'X used to make such good cars and now their standards have really dropped'. And these comments are made whether or not the car has been looked after to the manufacturer's instructions (top up the battery every three months, check the oil weekly, and so on). The HR world works in the same way: if the HR service runs smoothly – from a functional point of view – the best survey result will be neutral. But make one mistake and perceptions will turn negative overnight.

HR BPs frequently find themselves cast into a situation where, however good they are, they can never get beyond the nitty gritty and fire fighting. In other words, the HR engine is misfiring before they even start their new role.

Business people interviewed about their view of HR provide a consistent response:

- there is no doubt that most business people understand the potential value HR can bring;

- business people understand theoretically why the Business Partner model should be useful to them; but

- there is very little faith that the Business Partner theory can be made to work in practice if HR cannot get the basics right.

This may or may not be fair, but experience shows this is the way most business people think. The challenge is how to change this perception. And the answer, ironically, involves borrowing ideas that have been used for years in business to manage perceptions – in customer service call centres through to marketing departments – and this is what will be discussed in the next two sections of this chapter.

COMMON PITFALLS ENCOUNTERED WHEN INTRODUCING THE BUSINESS PARTNER MODEL

In implementing any change, the best place to study successes and failures is from the viewpoint of the end user or customer. Many business people look at the introduction of HR BPs in a somewhat jaundiced way before it has even begun. However, rather than being negative, this perception represents a huge opportunity for HR. Expectations are frequently very low – so it should not be too difficult to exceed them. There are a few mistakes that should be avoided at all costs which we will now discuss.

IGNORING THE BASICS

Over ten years ago BT made its first attempt to get into the lucrative systems integration business. This was seen as a vital part of their business strategy – partly because their core fixed-line business was under attack from new entrants, but also because the world of telecoms and networking was rapidly converging with information technology and this represented a clear business opportunity. However, every time a BT sales person tried to broach the subject of systems integration with their key customers, they were more often than not met with comments along the lines of 'I am not willing to talk to you about anything at all until you get my phone system working'. BT learned the lesson and have built a highly successful systems integration business, but only by ensuring that they got the basics working before they tried to sell 'higher end' services. The same is true of the HR BP. However good the individual Business Partner is, they do not stand a chance if HR does not have the infrastructure to get the basics right day in day out, year in and year out.

FAILURE TO SEE THE WHOLE PICTURE

This point builds on the one above. For an HR BP to be able to dedicate their time to doing the job properly, they need to have a simple interface back into the rest of HR. And they need to have the confidence that the HR 'back office' will do the job right. Unfortunately, many an HR BP initiative is an overlay on the existing HR organization or even just a rebadging of existing HR manager roles. The HR BP must have the time to dedicate to working with their business unit and this cannot be achieved unless their administration load is reduced through a reorganization of the whole HR department. Without looking at the effectiveness of the whole delivery model, efforts to achieve more Business Partnering will fail. Serious consideration needs to be given to reviewing options for centralizing and streamlining transactional support in a Shared Service and creating Centres of Excellence that ensure specialist knowledge and support is available when needed. This approach is now commonly referred to as 'HR transformation'.

POOR PROJECT MANAGEMENT

There comes a time in any transformation project when strategizing and planning comes to an end and the job of turning the plan into reality begins. This is a critical point, partly because this is where a large proportion of plans, ambitious or not, end up in a ring binder on a shelf somewhere gathering dust and partly because this is where the job gets difficult – or at least seems to. Why is this? Our research, carried out between 2003 and 2005, across more than 20 HR transformation projects shows that the answer is pretty obvious. It takes a particular set of skills to produce a convincing strategy and a detailed plan and a very different set of skills to actually turn that plan into a working operation. And this is where most people go wrong; they assume that the talented person who delivered the strategy and convinced the stakeholders is the right person to deliver the programme.

THE WRONG PEOPLE ARE APPOINTED AS BUSINESS PARTNERS

From a business point of view, the effective HR BP should be a core member of the management team, involved as much with the formulation and delivery of business strategy as the finance, operations or marketing person. It is clear, therefore, that the person should be of similar calibre to the others on the team and be capable of holding their own in that environment. Get this wrong and the credibility of the Business Partner strategy will be in tatters. In the same way that many finance managers could not step into the Finance Director's shoes, you should not expect most HR administration managers to be able to step into the HR BP role – and yet this is what happens in many organizations.

POOR COMMUNICATION WITH BUSINESS CUSTOMERS

The old adage about effective communication is that, to get your message across effectively, you should 'tell them what you are going to tell them, then tell them, then tell them what you have told them'. The same is true where you are trying to embed a message or change perceptions. The HR BP model can represent a fundamental shift in approach and should be the key both to transforming HR and the way it is perceived. Given that it is so important, the communication of the message as well as the marketing of the 'new look' HR should be taken very seriously. In most HR change programmes this is overlooked or promises are made and not kept.

These five points could apply to almost any major project but, despite this, it is surprising how frequently not just one of these mistakes is made, but all of them. Over and above these points the other message that comes loud and clear from the business is *keep it simple*. Yet too often the simple and logical concept of organizing your HR function to deliver best value is over-complicated in its implementation and this simply clouds the strategy and increases the likelihood of it going wrong.

WINNING THE HEARTS AND MINDS OF THE BUSINESS – A STRATEGY FOR SUCCESS

So far in this chapter we have looked at the business's overall perception of HR and what drives that perception. We have also discussed the common mistakes made when launching an HR BP programme. The final section of this chapter will pull this together into a practical strategy for laying good foundations with readers' business customers so that they are able to not only change the perception of HR across the business but also demonstrate that HR can add real value to the overall success of the business. If readers look back at the common mistakes discussed above, they will notice that these can be turned around into positive statements that together go a long way to ensuring success and winning the hearts and minds of the business:

- the HR BP programme must be part of a broader HR transformation programme;
- project management discipline is key;
- launch only when you are absolutely ready;
- be ruthless in your selection of HR BPs;
- be consistent, simple and clear when communicating to the business.

Clearly these are not the only 'rules' you need – you need clear objectives, a sound business case, alignment to the business strategy, and so on – but assuming that the

HR transformation programme is signed off and ready to roll, then these five rules will keep you on track and increase your chances of success. And most importantly, keep the business on your side.

Taking each of the points in turn:

THE HR BP PROGRAMME MUST BE PART OF AN HR TRANSFORMATION PROGRAMME

If your HR function is a well-oiled machine that delivers consistent and reliable service to the business then this may not apply to you. But if the reality is that HR managers spend most of their time fighting fires and doing administration, then trying to implement an HR BP model without any other change in the HR organization is metaphorically like putting lipstick on a pig. From a business perspective it is vital that the HR BP has free rein to really get into the business they support and become a real part of the management team. This can only be achieved if the day-to-day administration and management reporting is done by someone else. This implies, for most organizations, a radical rethink of how HR is structured and how it delivers service. The most important aspect of HR transformation is to create a clear separation between HR administration tasks and value-added strategic HR.

PROJECT MANAGEMENT DISCIPLINE IS KEY

HR is a complex part of the business and provides support to the business across the whole employee life-cycle – from 'attract' through to 'exit'. Even in a medium-sized organization, changing the way that those services are delivered requires careful planning and even more careful implementation. After all, there is no point in getting it half right, as this will only confirm the business's poor view of HR. A complex project requires competent management and this means that it absolutely must be run by someone with a track record of managing projects – projects that have delivered the required outcomes on time and to budget. HR knowledge may be useful but it is not essential.

LAUNCH ONLY WHEN YOU ARE ABSOLUTELY READY

A commonly held view is that the most loyal customers are created by 'under promising and over delivering'. In other words, when you set an expectation make sure you, at the very worst, meet the expectation but you should aim to beat it. Badly run projects have a habit of going off like a damp squib.

Imagine that you are a newly appointed HR BP. It is day one and the business has had clear simple communications about your role. And yet, in your first meeting with the management team of your business unit, you are drowned with complaints about HR administrative errors. You are in an impossible situation that is probably, from a business perspective, worse than under the traditional model. The service is no better but expectations have been raised. It's a bit like the BT example discussed at the beginning of this chapter. Do not launch until you are absolutely certain that you can deliver a marked change consistently and without error (95 per cent or more of the time, and for business-critical processes such as payroll, at least 99.9 per cent needs to be right first time).

BE RUTHLESS IN YOUR SELECTION OF HR BPs

The trouble with the HR BP role is that, on paper, it reads like every HR professional's ideal job – the reason that they embarked on a career in HR in the first place. But the job, in reality, requires very distinct skills that many HR people do not possess and some are unlikely to be able to learn. This is covered in detail in Chapter 13 but the point here is that compromises should not be made in the selection of Business Partners. It is again a case of meeting the expectation HR has set – HR BPs are part of the management team of a business adding value to the development and delivery of business strategy. You need to make absolutely sure that the people whom you put in these roles have the capability to deliver to your expectations otherwise the business will quickly mark this down as another 'nice try'.

BE CONSISTENT, SIMPLE AND CLEAR WHEN COMMUNICATING TO THE BUSINESS

HR has been slow to pick up on the power of marketing. The Group HRD of a major financial services business commented recently that it is frustrating that HR is seen as 'neutral' in his annual staff survey when they deliver exceptional services to the business (and they do). The only thing he had missed was to understand the need in this information-overloaded age to get out there and tell the business all about how great the HR function is. The risk of course is that he must be sure he can exceed any expectations that this communication creates.

The same is true of an HR BP initiative (whether it is part of an HR transformation programme or not). You have to get out there and tell people what to expect, how to use the service, what it doesn't do and so on. But whatever the message make sure you follow the three key rules of communication:

- tell them what you are going to tell them, then tell them, then tell them what you have told them;

- always under promise and over deliver;

- consistency and simplicity matter more than anything else.

To summarize, senior business people are acutely aware of the importance of strategic

HR but mainly because of HR's past record, most see their HR function as primarily delivering administration and not strategy. Anything that supports the business more effectively in the strategic HR area will undoubtedly be welcomed. But all initiatives coming from HR will have to overcome some resistance and scepticism. The only way to do this is for HR to get the basics right 95 per cent of the time – in a way this gives 'permission' to have the strategic conversation. Once the basics are right you then need to design the HR organization in such a way that the HR BP has the space and freedom to deliver on the strategic HR promises. And finally, you need to be absolutely sure that the individuals appointed into the Business Partner roles have the skills and experience to be able to deliver.

CHAPTER 12

Measurement for Success

Now tell me very slowly what it is you do …

Larry Ellison, CEO, Oracle Corporation

Oracle's HR Director for Europe, the Middle East, Africa and India, Vance Kearney, quoted Oracle's CEO Larry Ellison as saying 'Now tell me very slowly what it is you do …'.[1] HR has traditionally found this very difficult to do – or at least to do so in a way that is both valued and understood by the line. If HR BPs are not able provide a clear value statement that captures the business benefit they bring, they may be seen at best as a necessary evil and at worst as surplus to requirement. In a world where performance measurement is progressively more value based, HR needs its own language to articulate the value it brings. Managers are trained to work with numbers and, like it or not, numbers speak louder than words – so it is the effective quantification of that value that will really make the difference.

The provision of basic manpower data should be something that is firmly within the capability of any HR function, but it is frightening how few can testify to the seamless provision of accurate business information. The increasing adoption of improved HR technology has meant that many HR functions have made great strides in getting these basics right, but the danger still exists that this is where they will stop, and that the real 'so what's' that should take organizations beyond the data will not be addressed. If HR is to move up the value chain, it needs to be able to focus, measure and analyse the impact of its activities.

When discussing the topic of measuring contribution, it is important to distinguish between measuring the effectiveness of the HR function *per se* and HR's role in measuring the human dimension of an organization's performance. In this chapter we will examine the following topic areas:

- the value of measurement – why?
- measuring HR against human capital
- approaches to measurement
- measurement effectiveness
- measuring for success – what's next?

---

1   Orion Partners' Research 2003–04.

THE VALUE OF MEASUREMENT

Part 1 of this book highlighted the changes that have affected the traditional HR function. e-HR, shared services and outsourcing are fundamentally transforming much of the transactional activity that was once HR's heartland. In theory this has been a positive step for the function, releasing the space and resources it needs to intervene at the strategic level. However, expecting the business to respond differently to HR just because it has decided to 'be more strategic' is a wish unlikely to be fulfilled. In a world that is ever hungrier for information, managers want proof and this means numbers. For organizations to recognize the value that a transformed HR function can deliver, they need to be able to measure the way in which the function contributes to the achievement of organizational objectives. Effective measurement allows for an evaluation of the degree of alignment between functional and organizational strategies and helps identify those areas that should be the focus for change. Quantifying what is important and then assessing levels of achievement should be standard practice, but when the assets being managed are intangible and the interventions often soft in nature, this is no easy task. Indeed, in a survey carried out by the Corporate Leadership Council[2], the HR executives surveyed felt that only a third of the metrics managed by HR were genuinely linked to their organizations' objectives.

In their work *The HR Scorecard*[3], Becker, Huselid and Ulrich also recognized the challenge, claiming that one of the most critical actions HR can take is to develop a measurement system that captures the impact the function has on the business. They provide guidance and support as to how an organization might develop such a framework, but still acknowledge that the aspiration of a balanced scorecard that covers all elements of an organization's HR performance may be too challenging at the outset and that an initial focus on the HR function itself may be a more achievable objective. Even at this level, this means much more than providing evidence to justify one's existence – actually quantifying to the line, in language they understand, the bottom-line value that HR can add.

MEASURING HUMAN CAPITAL

The statement that 'people are our most important asset' has been used so frequently that it may now seem almost meaningless or certainly lacking in sincerity when it is made. However, in an economy burnt by the smoke and mirrors of the dot com boom, placing a value on what is real has become increasingly important. As other sources of competitive advantage prove increasingly difficult to sustain growing emphasis has been focused on quantifying the value of human capital. From EMI Music to Oracle,

---

2 Corporate Leadership Council (2002) *Metrics Survey*.
3 *The HR Scorecard. Linking People, Strategy, and Performance* (2001) Becker, B.E., Huselid, M.A. and Ulrich, D. Boston: Harvard Business School Press.

from the Prudential to The Football Association, the HR Directors interviewed for this book stressed their belief in the increasing value of the distinctive capabilities of each of their workforces. Having said this, almost all of those interviewed also admitted that there was very little quantitative or qualitative measurement of HR's role in building these capabilities. At a basic level, most organizations measured employee satisfaction, with some taking this further to assess the degree of employees' alignment to organizational or corporate brand values.[4] However, the primary measurement focus within most of the organizations with whose representatives we talked was still cost and headcount data.

As well as the earlier works by Becker and Huselid, many more studies have sought to find the most effective mechanisms for measuring human capital. Within the UK, studies carried out by individuals and institutions alike[5] have identified the challenges of evaluating human capital. The subject was the topic of a government consultation document, entitled *Accounting for People*, issued in May 2003 by the Task Force on Human Capital Management.[6] The paper sought to do the following:

- review the performance measures currently used to assess organizations' investment in human capital;

- consider the best practices in reporting and provide an assessment of those that are most valuable to stakeholders;

- establish and champion the business case for investing in reporting on human capital.

As a result, since April 2005, annual reports produced by 1300 publicly quoted British companies must be accompanied by operating and financial reviews including relevant details on how investment in employee development might affect future business performance. Regulators, fearful of becoming too prescriptive, have given companies leeway to choose what to report, in part because it is so difficult to develop common measures for people management across diverse industries. A recent study by the Chartered Management Institute[7] found that, although 90 per cent of managers had attempted to measure the contribution of employees to business performance, 'only 20 per cent thought their measures were effective or even useful'. The new reporting requirements clearly have limited power, but the very fact that the notion of measuring the value of human capital is now a formal requirement proves the need for HR to be able to lead the debate rather than merely follow it from the sidelines.

---

4   Accenture, BSkyB.
5   David Guest, Andrew Mayo, The Work Foundation and the CIPD.
6   DTI (2003) *Accounting for People* Consultation Paper, May. www.accountingforpeople@dti.gsi.gov.uk
7   *Financial Times* (2005) 'Doubt Over New Reporting Requirement', 1 April.

A COMMON LANGUAGE FOR MEASUREMENT

In the absence of central standards like those in the accountancy profession, a common language for measurement is starting to emerge through the introduction of global benchmarking tools developed by bodies such as EP-First & Saratoga and consultancies like Watson Wyatt. The EP-First & Saratoga benchmarks focus primarily on the quantitative measurement of the HR function in terms of size and cost. However, as with all benchmark data, irrespective of the precision of the definitions, there can be a danger of comparing apples with pears. A business's organizational culture and specific requirements will have a major influence on its cost drivers and so any comparative measurement across organizations within the same industry, or of a similar size, needs to be undertaken with caution.

Tools like Watson Wyatt's Human Capital Index[8] seek to provide more qualitative data, assessing the business impact of effective human capital practices. The Watson Wyatt HCI survey now covers 1500 major companies, across a wide range of sectors and geographies. It clearly demonstrates the value added by a strong people management capability – stating a figure of 89.6 per cent value added – where the difference in shareholder value created relates to the difference in the effectiveness of human capital management. Categories of human capital management practice they identify include clarity of rewards and accountability (21.5 per cent value added), integrity of communications (7 per cent value added) and prudent use of resources (14.5 per cent value added).

From the HR function's perspective, an important finding is also the impact of the effectiveness of HR itself, which has been measured as having a 21 per cent impact on value added. The survey subsequently divides the area of HR functional effectiveness into three key areas: business alignment (7.2 per cent value added), cost effectiveness (9.6 per cent value added) and the focused use of HR service technology (4.2 per cent value added).

APPROACHES TO MEASUREMENT

Having discussed the importance of measurement and reviewed some of its key dimensions, both quantitative and qualitative, we must now turn to actual practice. This book is intended to cover the broader topic of the role of the HR Business Partner, so does not offer a detailed review of all the measurement practices in operation today. However, we are able to reflect on the approaches used in the wide group of organizations whose HR Directors we interviewed, as well as the knowledge and

---

8   Watson Wyatt (2002) *Human Capital Index*.

understanding gained from our own consulting experience. In the context of assessing the HR BP role, the key requirement is that we evaluate how measurement practices can help embed and reinforce a role that still appears, too frequently, to have been limited in its real impact.

MEASURING THE FUNCTION – A SCORECARD APPROACH

The concept of the balanced scorecard seeks to capture a comprehensive picture of the performance of a specific function and will normally cover the strategic, customer, operations and financial dimensions. It should provide visible linkage of the function's contribution to the organization's strategic objectives and, if implemented effectively, should form a natural sub-set of the corporate balanced scorecard. At its most sophisticated level, the high performance work system, described in *The HR Scorecard*[9] should aim to adopt as comprehensive a definition of HR as possible. Making the transition from no measurement to measuring all dimensions of an organization's human performance is a challenging one, and so a scorecard that starts with the performance of the function itself will often be a major step forward.

How to develop an HR scorecard

The first step in developing a scorecard is to translate the strategy into specific key result areas (KRAs). KRAs will:

- identify the areas which are key to successfully meeting strategic objectives;
- represent the desired goals and objectives of the function;
- translate the strategy into clear action points;
- asks the question 'What action must we take in order to meet our strategic objectives?'.

Once KRAs are identified, key performance indicators (KPIs) should then be established. Each KPI should represent the best indicator of performance for a specific KRA, and every KRA should have at least one measure. KPIs will:

- be quantifiable measures for evaluating progress towards the accomplishment of goals;
- answer the question 'How do we measure success?';
- be SMART – Specific, Measurable, Actionable, Relevant, Timely;
- not be too numerous!

9   *The HR Scorecard. Linking People, Strategy, and Performance* (2001) Becker, B.E., Huselid, M.A. and Ulrich, D. Boston: Harvard Business School Press.

Once the KPIs have been established, performance standards must be determined for each measure. The performance standards represent the ideal level of performance.

- Tracking a performance measure over time shows whether things are getting better or worse.

- Simply knowing that an area is improving is usually not enough. An improvement needs to be compared to a performance standard.

- Performance standards measure the level of success, and even failure, in attaining a goal.

Table 12.1 Example of a balanced scorecard

Dimensions	KRAs	KPIs	Performance standards
Strategic	• Attraction and retention of talent • Building of strategic capabilities • Clearly defined culture and values • Provision of strategic management information	• Retention of high performers • Development of core programmes • Accurate and timely provision of management information	• 95% new hires retention after 6 months • 90% skills attainment • 85% employee satisfaction • % accuracy and turnaround time
Customer	• Partner with business • Provide responsive quality service	• Customer satisfaction rates	• 80% time spent with executives • 90% customer satisfaction
Operations	• Optimization of HR services through service delivery model	• Volume per delivery channel • Cost per transaction • Average cycle times	• % query resolution by channel • 95% self-service take-up
Financial	• Maximization of human capital performance • Minimization of HR costs	• HR ROI • HR cost per FTE	• 1% HR cost to revenue • £1000 per employee head • 0.5% budget variance

Source: Orion Partners (2003).

FINANCIAL MEASURES

Many of the HRDs we interviewed admitted to focusing primarily on two of the four dimensions of the scorecard – financial and operational. Irrespective of an organization's sector, cost pressures have undoubtedly been at the heart of the HR agenda in recent years and many HRDs cited the critical role that HR had played in managing the cost base with highly detailed breakdowns of headcount cost information. At Cable & Wireless, the HRD talked about the level of financial measurement expected from each HR BP:

> *At a time like this* [one of turmoil in the telecommunications sector]
> *there are a whole host of tangible measures where HR adds to the bottom
> line. I expect each of my senior Business Partners to share the financial
> objectives of the business unit they support – they need to understand
> the opex* [operational expenditure] *and have to manage the margin
> implications of all those activities that impact headcount costs.*

At Oracle, Vance Kearney painted a similar picture:

> *In the last couple of years, we have been purely measured on our ability
> to cut cost – cost per head. However, I can see that starting to change. The
> emphasis will still be financial, but will be on productivity – revenue
> generated per head …*

OPERATIONAL MEASURES

In recent years, a number of factors have increased the level of sophistication of the
measurement of HRD operations. Our discussions with HRDs at organizations such as
the Prudential, Accenture, Tui and Deutsche Bank, found the primary focus of
measurement activity was here – with large quantities of data being produced to
support the speed and efficiency of HR processing. Technology has clearly played a
major role; improved access to data and the introduction of employee and manager
self-service in many organizations have meant that core HR data are more widely
available than ever before. External benchmarking like that provided by EP-First &
Saratoga has also given the profession a series of ratios by which to measure itself.
These have meant that any self-respecting HRD would be embarrassed not to know
how their function compared in size and cost to others in their sector.

Another major development has been the increase in outsourcing, which has
brought with it its own contractual language of measurement – the service levels which
are to be met for contractual obligations to be fulfilled. This change is equally true of
organizations who have established their own internal Shared Services organizations,
where the relationship with the rest of the HR function is akin to that with an
outsourcer, though without the contractual obligations. This in itself is a positive force
for increasing the level of measurement. Organizations that have outsourced any part
of their HR processes should be able to expect detailed service performance reporting
as part of the outsourcing arrangements.

In an outsourced arrangement, monthly performance reporting not only provide
the Business Partner community with data relating to contractual performance,
volumes of transactions processed or calls taken to helplines. They should also analyse
trends in the underlying drivers of those transactions that will assist the retained HR

function in prioritizing HR activities. If used effectively, this information should be used as part of the overall picture provided to the line of the organization's HR performance. Interestingly, this is where HR BPs are under pressure to perform. In our conversations with the HR outsourcing provider Xchanging's Alan Bailey, he commented:

> *The pressure has been on from the retained HR functions to provide more and more performance data on the outsourced services. We are now able to provide highly sophisticated reporting which captures the key metrics for both the in-house and outsourced components of many of the HR processes. Managers have this information and what's interesting is that they're cottoning onto the fact that this only represents half the story – they get detailed information on the transactional components – but how are the Business Partners measuring what they're delivering?*

CUSTOMER MEASURES

Although a fundamental dimension of the performance assessment of most organizations, the notion of customer satisfaction is still relatively new to the HR function. Measurement of employee satisfaction has become a regular feature of HR activity – with a whole industry of surveys producing statistics on employees' reactions to their employers' efforts to provide a 'great place to work'. Cynics amongst us may question how relevant this may be, when staff may just be grateful to have a place to work … However, many large and well-respected organizations – B&Q, Pepsico and Tesco to name but a few[10] – have made major investments in programmes to measure employee satisfaction levels, believing it to be a significant contributor to overall business performance. In evaluating the value of human capital, it is undoubtedly a major factor, but the notion of managers and employees as customers of the HR function is slightly different.

Seeing HR as a provider of services valued by its customers implies that the customer has been consulted and also that they have a choice. This is not wholly the case in HR, as it is unlikely that customers have much of a say in how they receive its services although they may have the freedom to find alternative suppliers should their company's procurement processes allow them to do so. The notion of consultation is probably more pertinent as it points yet again to the HR function's ability to develop 'services' and 'products' – and yes, this is often the language used – without any regard to whether the business and the end users within that business actually need or want what is being offered.

---

10   The Human Resources Forum, May (2003) www.richmondevents.com

STRATEGIC MEASURES – PREDICTING THE FUTURE

Turning finally to the strategic dimension of the scorecard is not to say that it is the least important area to measure. On the contrary, HR's ability to measure its contribution to the longer-term strategic goals of an organization is critical in its efforts to fulfil the role of strategic partner. Too frequently HR is the valiant workhorse that deals with the aftermath of others' strategic thinking or just stays focused on the challenges of delivering today's service. A keen eye to the organization's future needs – most typically in the areas of talent identification and leadership development – will be what differentiates an HR function that merely copes, from one that helps drive the strategic agenda.

CASE STUDY: Major investment bank – measuring capability for the future

At a major investment bank, the bank's Global Head of Strategic Solutions and Business Programmes was able to provide us with an impressively pragmatic example of an approach his organization had taken to measuring human capital.

Instigated to meet the need to increase the level of its staff's competence, in a newly competitive market, he and a small project team developed a series of competency-based role profiles and role families to cover all the functions in the bank. Nothing new in this, you might say, but the distinctive feature of the 'Role Define' programme was the way in which these role profiles have been directly linked to a series of tangible business outputs.

The team started by working with the business to define what was required. The critical component was that they were now able to measure performance and gather data that relate directly to the needs of the business. Strikingly, the teams in the front line came to HR to help them with business planning, as the performance data generated through this model enable a concrete assessment of the capability of an individual or a team and help to identify the levers that will predict superior performance. This initiative has also helped the HR function to adapt other key processes in the spheres of learning and development and compensation and benefits.

In a good news story where HR has added significant value, there are lessons to be learnt about the capability requirements of HR BPs. The challenge in really driving through and sustaining this model has not been in the capability and the attitude of the line, but in developing the business skills of the client relationship managers, the bank's HR BPs. Critical to cementing the linkages between competence and output has been the HR BPs' ability to understand not just the skills and behavioural dimension, but also the fundamentals of the business they are in.

THE EFFECTIVENESS OF HR MEASUREMENT

It is important that we assess how effective HR functions are in measuring contribution. Throughout this chapter, we have stressed that the key achievement of an effective measurement framework is its ability to articulate the value added by the function. The word on which to focus in the previous sentence is *effective* – by which we mean focused, tangible and relevant. Unfortunately, despite the plethora of measurement data and statistics produced by many HR functions, those that are relevant to the business they support and are communicated in a language they understand are few and far between.

In 2002 the Corporate Leadership Council carried out a survey amongst its members to assess the use of HR data and metrics in business decision-making.[11] The survey identified five core groups of metrics relating to:

- *Return on Investment (ROI)/impact metrics:* Measures that capture the ROI or impact of HR activities on improvements in business performance, HR performance or workforce performance (for example ROI of training, correlation between competitiveness of compensation package and employee turnover).

- *Effectiveness Metrics:* Measures of productivity, speed and levels of performance of the workforce and HR (for example productivity, strength of employment brand, quality of training content).

- *Satisfaction Metrics:* Measures of line manager or workforce satisfaction in terms of the importance that they place on one item compared with another (for example a line manager's satisfaction with new hires, employees' satisfaction with benefits-related transactions).

- *Volume Metrics:* Measures designed to capture the frequency of workforce or HR activities (for example rate of absenteeism, average number of hours employees spend in training per year, turnover of new hires).

- *Cost Metrics:* Measure of individual and aggregate costs of workforce or HR activities (for example the total operating cost of the HR function, total training cost, cost of turnover).

Clear differences were distinguished between the categories of information that were valued by the different audiences who received it, notably, 'ROI/impact' scored 53 per cent with the CEO group as opposed to 9 per cent with HR staff, whilst 'Volume' scored 8 per cent with CEOs against 30 per cent with HR. The survey also assessed the

---

11 Chapter 1. *State of the Membership. Utilizing HR Metrics for Business Decision Making.* Corporate Executive Board 2002.

effectiveness of HR metrics in supporting businesses in their decision-making. Participating organizations were asked to rank specific business objectives by their level of importance and then to assess how effective HR metrics were for those business objectives[12].

Table 12.2   Gap between importance and effectiveness of business decision support

Rank order 1–13, by size of gap

Business objective	% of organizations rating as 'important' or 'very important' to support	% of organizations rating themselves as 'effective' or 'very effective'	Gap between importance and effectiveness
1. Forecasting talent needs to optimize recruiting	83.2	16.8	66.4
2. Ensuring HR process efficiency	91.4	32.9	58.5
3. Improving managers' effectiveness at people management	87.8	30.4	57.4
4. Measuring the performance/potential of employees against development objectives and/or job requirements	83.9	27.5	56.1
5. Managing succession planning	81.0	25.5	55.5
6. Ensuring the efficiency of the internal labour market	75.8	22.1	53.7
7. Calibrating the strength of the leadership bench	80.3	27.9	52.4
8. Aligning training and development with organizational needs	84.1	32.4	51.7
9. Driving customer service	73.5	25.2	48.3
10. Driving HR process re-engineering	74.7	27.5	47.2
11. Ensuring quality of hire	80.8	34.2	46.6
12. Improving the strength of the employment brand	64.9	19.0	45.9
13. Aligning efforts to retain the right staff with organizational needs	87.4	42.3	45.1

Interestingly, organizations ranked themselves as effective in only three objectives that they considered important: controlling HR costs, ensuring employee satisfaction and managing downsizing initiatives. The three objectives for which HR organizations reported they were least likely to provide effective measurement support were forecasting talent needs to optimize recruitment, ensuring joint venture success and screening alliance partners for cultural compatibility. The first three are not unimportant in themselves, but they indicate that HR is still working at the operational rather than strategic level.

---

12   Corporate Leadership Council (2002)*Metrics Survey.*

To add insult to injury, one of the objectives rated as being most important by HR functions – ensuring HR process efficiency – has one of the most significant gaps between importance and effectiveness. This suggests that, despite its importance, most of those responding to the survey feel that the function is not delivering. If this is what we have referred to in this and other chapters as 'getting the basics right', there still appears to be a way to go, even if this is only in terms of perception. It is the gap between what organizations need and the way in which they are leveraging the information provided by HR that is most concerning.

HR functions that were ranked as both effective and ineffective in intent seemed to share the same goals, as well as similar challenge:

- identification of meaningful metrics
- lack of supporting infrastructure
- lack of skills amongst HR staff
- assigning accountability for metrics
- making measurement information available to the people who need it.

The difference between those organizations classified as effective and ineffective seems to lie less in what they hoped to measure and the challenges they faced in implementing a system for measurement, but more in the execution. Those organizations that were characterized as effective had greater confidence in the link of measures to corporate performance. They also cited higher levels of utilization of measures, which would tend to suggest that the measures they had in place had more currency in their organizations and were more ingrained in the way business gets done.

MEASURING FOR SUCCESS

For an activity to become part of the 'way things gets done round here', it needs to have certain characteristics.

LANGUAGE OF THE LINE

We have already commented on the importance of language. Too often the HR function gets wrapped up in its own mystique, over-intellectualizing to an extent that means common-sense approaches get lost in jargon. Any attempts to measure HR's contribution need to be communicated in a language its customers will understand.

DEMONSTRATE LINKAGE TO PROFITABILITY

There is little point in HR measuring aspects that no one outside their function cares about. Too many measures focus on peripheral aspects of activities such as the percentage of performance appraisals completed by line managers. If there is no clear linkage between the completion of an appraisal and the application of a reward or a consequence to the employee for over- or underperformance then the measurement is not really meaningful. Measures that support the underlying customer orientation of the organization or encourage service delivery to exacting standards are likely to be much more useful.

DEMONSTRATE FLEXIBILITY

Measurement systems only add value when they can measure what matters. Criteria that are business critical at one point can be irrelevant six months later. As such it is important that the approach allows for the flexibility to adapt to changing priorities. A good solution is often a core group of standard measures that are universally applicable, with the opportunity to add specific measures that allow for monitoring particular 'hot issues'.

CHAPTER 13

Capabilities for Successful Business Partnering

*The first way to an easy life is to be c**p. If you're skills aren't relevant,
then neither are you and the business will get on without you …*

Executive Vice President HR, global software company

Parts 1 and 2 of this book have sought to provide insight into the structural and technological changes that have impacted the HR function. We have seen that the emergence of new delivery models has shifted the emphasis of the generalist role. Transactional activity has been automated and centralized, and specialist skills have been concentrated in Centres of Excellence, leaving a very different role for the HR professional in the line. Structure is one thing, but the key to successful delivery lies in the skills to execute. It is our belief that it is in managing this equation that HR has failed to maximize its opportunity. Now more than ever, people management is seen as a business-enabling discipline. Line managers have 'got' the principle that the way an organization manages and develops its people can change the way it functions and have a direct impact on its success. The ownership of those processes should lie with the line. For HR to establish and embed its role in shaping the strategy, it needs credibility.

HR is still a long way from automatically being credible. In the past, credibility may have come from fear – the 'cop' element of the 'cop vs. prop' expression sometimes used to describe the function of HR. It is unlikely to have come from the 'prop' component of the HR role – although many managers might often have been only too pleased to relinquish the ownership of difficult people issues to a willing HR helper, this would generally have earnt the HR function gratitude rather than respect. Unfortunately, we suspect that the skills associated with HR still lie predominantly in these areas of helping people with the basics, rather than in those of strategic thinking, business insight and change management.

WHAT IS THE CHANGE?

Looking back at Part 1 a number of key themes stand out that drive HR's move away from its traditional skills and competencies. HR now finds itself looking at the following changed areas of focus:

- the rise of alternative sourcing models for HR services (both internal and externally provided);

- interaction with the financial and strategic analysis of the business's aims and objectives;

- the implementation of sophisticated HRIS systems that are changing the administration, methods of employee interaction and management information around HR activities;

- a higher profile for and central role in strategic analysis and execution;

- the requirement for detailed planning and evaluation;

- the reliance on non-HR team and resources to deliver results.

Traditionally, however, the competencies of HR professionals were based around the delivery of a service, very much in the core HR professional or functional arena. These competencies included the knowledge and delivery of traditional HR services such as reward/compensation, employee relations training and development, organizational design, employee relations and compliance with increasingly complex legislation. In these areas functional specialism has been prized and has arguably been a 'hiding place' for practitioners. The mystique of policy interpretation, vagaries of employment law and the confidential nature of many HR issues has created a place that is HR's alone and has given it the grounds to validate its existence without recourse to engaging with the business and its objectives.

HR practitioners' and managers' expectation of HR are that it is operational or administrative and, by implication, inward looking. The HR BP must be not just the HR expert but also a Strategic Partner and Change Agent. The new approach of HR Business Partnership would move HR from an inward-looking to a strategic role, serving the business by anticipating and addressing its needs. This means it is necessary to propose another capability model for HR professionals, to enable HR to become consultants to managers, and the competencies required to do this will be very different.

In this chapter we would like to propose a simple skills framework for the successful HR BP. It has been developed as a result of the extensive work we have carried out with high-performing HR executives. It attempts to describe a potential role model, with examples of approaches that we have identified as achieving tangible results.

THE IMPORTANCE OF CONTEXT

Before we outline the skills framework in more detail we should reflect a moment on the importance of context. In our experience, the skills we have identified in the framework can be applied across all industries. Our research (Orion Partners, 2003–05) enabled us to test our theories in many different environments, from FMCG to telecommunications, financial services to oil and gas, and public sector to professional services. The one thing that does differ, however, and which plays a critical role in the effective deployment of any skills framework, is context. Although the skill groupings are common, it is an individual's ability to find the correct emphasis in any given context that will determine their level of success. Slavishly implementing those approaches considered 'best practice', irrespective of the organizational culture and climate, may at best be futile and at worst counter-productive.

A common thread in our discussions with the executives we interviewed was the notion of organizational maturity. Many had worked for a fairly diverse group of companies and yet were quickly at ease managing the different people challenges faced by the different organizations they had worked for. The concept of maturity implies an organization's ability to accept more or less sophisticated approaches; if an organization is not 'mature', it suggests that it is less receptive to change. In our conversations, what was critical to success was the sense and knowledge of where an organization was at, and the chameleon-like ability to identify and hone those areas where one's skills would have most impact.

BUSINESS GENERALIST VS TECHNICAL EXPERT

As outlined above, the key shift in emphasis in the Business Partner role is from technical expert to business generalist. When we look at the role in detail, the outcomes expected of the successful Business Partner are more akin to those of an internal consultant. However, we must be careful not to let the pendulum swing too far, as an understanding of the technical components of what makes a successful people agenda will still be vital. One way of looking at the role is to describe the role in terms of a T-shape consultant (see Figure 13.1).

A common way of defining the skills required of a successful consultant is to group together the generic skills required by all consultants across the top bar of the T. These would include relationship building, diagnosis, solution shaping and so on. This is then underpinned by a deep 'spike' of content skills that a consultant would bring to bear in their specific area of expertise, be it industry or functionally based. For the HR BP this part of the T would include the HR-specific knowledge and expertise required for their role. The important point to make here is that in the context of an HR delivery model that incorporates a Shared Services component for transactional activity and a Centre of Excellence approach to policy development, the key is for HR BPs to know how to access technical expertise rather than necessarily having it themselves – *knowing what you don't know, and knowing someone who does know.*

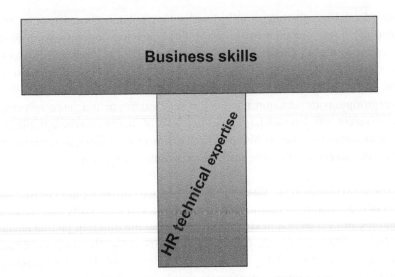

Source: Orion Partners (2004) *Achieving Excellence as a Business Partner*

Figure 13.1   The T-shaped consultant

BUSINESS PARTNER AS INTERNAL CONSULTANT

We regularly run workshops for teams of aspiring Business Partners and ask them to outline the key attributes and behaviours they expect from effective consultants with whom they have worked. They say that an effective consultant is someone who:

- 'understands my business in detail';
- 'brings insight from broader experience';
- 'challenges my thinking';
- 'drives through clarity in complex situations';
- 'manages stakeholders well and identifies change blockers';
- 'delivers on time and to budget'.

Participants on our workshops are quick to identify that these are exactly the kinds of skills they require as HR BPs, but for many this is a very new way of thinking about their role. Although the language may differ from organization to organization, the core competencies are very similar. We have found the model illustrated in Figure 13.2 a very useful way of summarizing these capabilities, and an example competency framework that provides sample descriptors can be found in Table 13.1 on page 134.

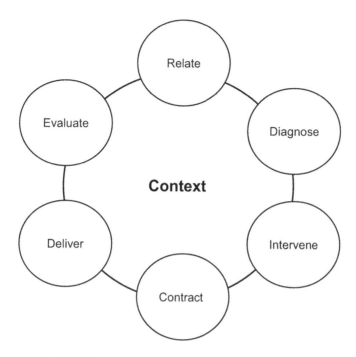

Source: Orion Partners (2004)

Figure 13.2   A consultancy framework

We will now examine each of the competencies in the framework in turn.

RELATE

Relationship management, by its very nature, involves understanding the needs and objectives of many different parties, internal and external and at all levels. It then requires the delivery of solutions to meet them to achieve aligned objectives.

Although relationship management is not defined or shaped by any real hierarchy, most HR functions tend to operate within a hierarchical environment and may continue to do so if that is the culture of the organization they serve. Regardless of this, the HR BP must develop true relationship management skills and operate outside that structure. A further challenge may be that they must, because of the very hierarchical nature of their organization, do this without seeming to!

The real challenge lies less in developing the skill of relationship management, and more in the environment where it is used. Knowing how to assess stakeholders' objectives, personal perspectives, motives and operating context is essential. Applying this knowledge to deliver results is the real goal.

DIAGNOSE

There are two types of diagnostic skills which are pertinent to the HR BP – one hard, one soft. The hard skill is demonstrating a sound grasp of the business and the financial drivers that underpin an organization's success. The soft is the ability to read between the lines and diagnose some of the more subtle people dimensions that affect performance. The HR BP cannot switch off in briefings about finance, strategy, marketing, technology, operations, customers, competitors, service and other business functions. They must understand each functional area well enough to be able to debate and provide alternative solutions to its HR-based problems. More importantly, they must be able to speak the language of these areas if they are to build the credibility to engage with their business counterparts. Like it or not the language of the finance and operations functions is the language of business today. Unless HR professionals know and understand the business and can contribute meaningfully to top-level business discussions they will not be invited to the top table. Knowing and understanding the business is fundamental to making HR's contribution more relevant.

HR professionals must become skilled at quantifying the impact of change in financial and other qualitative terms. HR BPs need to become more adept at presenting and tracking the case for change with formal business cases in terms of costs, volumes and satisfaction levels, and using these to predict the future. As each back-office function becomes leaner, the wins become harder and the investment cash for change more keenly fought over.

INTERVENE

Understanding the business strategy is one thing, but where the HR BP really begins to add value is in identifying the interventions that will ensure the people management priorities are aligned to deliver on that strategy. Anticipating ahead of time and being able to see the key interdependencies during the planning process will help the Business Partner to influence and shape the agenda rather than merely respond to it.

CONTRACT

Once there is clarity around the HR solutions that are required, it is then the Business Partner's responsibility to scope the necessary activity, and confirm deliverables and associated resourcing requirements. In an environment where the majority of delivery resources sit within either a Shared Services function or a Centre of Excellence, this will more than likely mean 'contracting' with in-house resources to deliver. Although this may not require some of the commercial disciplines associated with managing third parties, similar rigour is required. Often this will mean a shift for HR BPs who will need to adjust to focusing on managing 'outputs' rather than managing the process which delivers the outputs. Where this is extended to delivery via a third party, Business Partners will also need to develop the commercial acumen to manage these relationships effectively. Although it may be tempting to leave this to a procurement professional, the Business Partner's active participation in the management of the supplier relationship will always deliver a better result.

DELIVER

It is in this area that HR BPs can learn from their colleagues in project management. This is not about using flash gant charts and having an intimate knowledge of Microsoft Project, but managing multiple streams of activity to a defined milestone plan. Having scoped activity and agreed a defined set of outputs or deliverables with their clients, HR professionals must know how to make things happen themselves and how to help others manage change. They must be able to design a change process for both HR initiatives (such as how to implement a competency-based pay programme) and business initiatives (such as how to implement an innovation strategy).

Being able to see where change is needed and to design and implement effective solutions delivers value because strategies become realities and produce results. To be a professional partner in the business, HR must know how to translate a vision into reality. This cycle of change will not end once the model has been implemented as the model's purpose is to continue to drive change through continuous improvement of business performance. Developing real project management skills is essential.

Change skills must go beyond simply understanding the mechanics of managing change. Skills to influence the business to buy in to the change programme must be present. The stakeholder analysis and management related to this will be essential as HR raises its head more and more above the parapet, proposing business change through an organization's people. These are business-wide initiatives that will have a very high profile. Not all will be keen to see HR take this role, or to follow, and the HR practitioner will need the political skills to manage and overcome such obstacles.

EVALUATE

We have already spent an entire chapter reviewing the importance of measuring HR's contribution to the business. This discussion was at an organizational rather than an individual level, but the key principles still apply when identifying the 'must have' skill set for the HR BP. In the same way as comfort with numerical analysis will be important to a Business Partner's ability to diagnose key business issues, understanding return on investment and methods for tracking benefits realization will ensure they assess the value of HR's interventions. The key as always will be in the HR BP's ability to measure the business impact and communicate this in the language of the line.

Table 13.1   Example: HR capability framework

Business Partner Generic Capabilities	
RELATE – Build and maintain effective relationships with stakeholders	• Engage with line as client • Talk their language • Identify all key stakeholders • Recognize stakeholders' styles and adapt own style accordingly • Influence at all levels • Understand how to remove barriers with all stakeholders • Operate effectively in a matrix environment • Establish and maintain contacts internally and externally
DIAGNOSE – Identify and diagnose issues through a variety of techniques including interpreting management information and observing behaviours	• Make effective links between HR and business strategy • Analyse management information to diagnose business/organization/people issues • Demonstrate awareness of commercial issues and key interdependencies • Take a concept and make it real • Identify issues by watching and interpreting behaviour • Facilitate meetings to determine issues • Challenge the thinking and perceptions of the client
INTERVENE – Intervene at appropriate times, informing and influencing the business agenda	• Identify critical business issues and anticipate interventions required • Influence and shape the agenda • Develop structured conclusions, recommendations and implementation strategies • Identify blockers and develop strategies to overcome issues
CONTRACT – Develop HR plans that are fully aligned to business goals, and contract with all stakeholders about the delivery of HR advice and services	• Help the business develop strategic and operational plans • Contract with clients concerning scope deliverables, timetables, resources and costs • Align business and HR plans • Develop feasibility studies/business cases including benefits to the business • Ensure expectations are clear and service standards are agreed • Identify and source appropriate delivery resources
DELIVER – Deliver to agreed timelines ensuring business objectives are met	• Work effectively with stakeholders to resolve problems jointly • Own and deliver agreed outputs • Apply project management techniques • Organize time to work across multiple requirements

cont

	• Monitor and track plans
	• Ensure delivery against plans
	• Identify and escalate risks
EVALUATE – Continually monitor performance levels and track and evaluate the benefits of all HR-related initiatives	• Monitor performance against clear milestones
	• Quantify the business value of services/outputs delivered
	• Oversee related programmes identifying synergies and leveraging benefits
	• Share knowledge and ensure stakeholders and HR learn from successes and failures

To summarize, the skill set of the successful HR Business Partner should now be more closely aligned to that of an effective consultant (see Table 13.1). Whilst technical skills are still important and will provide customers with a degree of confidence in the people management specifics of the roles, they must be married with broader business consulting skills. If this is the case, the professional development routes traditionally followed by individuals aspiring to the role should be carefully examined and radically overhauled. Chapter 14 looks at how this might be achieved, from both a development and a career management perspective.

Developing the HR BP

If the role of the HR BP is now clear and the skills requirements well articulated, it is time for us to turn to the development approaches that can be used. There will be no surprises in learning that a combination of formal skills development, knowledge acquisition and experience is what is required. The difference is that the development path will look very different from that traditionally followed by most senior HR professionals.

The typical HR career development programme has traditionally focused on the refreshing of technical knowledge. Activities included attending functional seminars, completing a professional qualification – the Chartered Institute of Personnel Development (CIPD) qualification in the UK or Society of Human Resource Management (SHRM) qualifications in the US – and finally rotation through key HR areas of specialism. Interaction with the business was often limited and an holistic view of the skills and competencies needed was often lacking. Although we have seen ample evidence of an acknowledgement that the traditional HR skill set needs to change, the development route for individuals joining the profession appears to have remained largely unchanged. In the discussions we had with senior HR executives, it appeared that the pace of change often is being forced on HR from outside, by an osmosis of skills brought by individuals joining from other business disciplines. These executives appeared disappointed and dissatisfied with the relevance of the 'official' professional development available, while acknowledging that the broader sphere of management education had more to offer. This chapter goes on to explore the kind of activities that exist in each of the key areas of activity for the HR BP roles.

DEVELOPING CAPABILITY

As illustrated in Figure 14.1, effective capability development requires an individual to acquire a combination of skills, knowledge and experience. How much the onus to do this depends upon the individual and how much upon the organization will differ from company to company, but the individual must have the desire to succeed and this must be reinforced by positive role modelling from their leaders. Sadly, in our experience, there is often insufficient role modelling and this means that structured attempts at Business Partner development achieve less than they might. If managers within an HR function are not exhibiting the desired behaviours and demonstrating the right skill set, this will obviously have an impact on the effectiveness of other

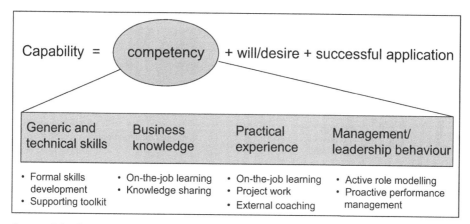

Source: Orion Partners (2004) *Delivering Excellence as a Business Partner*

Figure 14.1   Effective capability development

development activity. Yet again this points to the need to view any HR transformation activity from an holistic perspective: you cannot attempt to 'fix' one component without due consideration of other factors.

SKILLS DEVELOPMENT

Chapter 13 proposed a capability framework that combined technical HR skills with generic business consulting skills. Organizations differ in their approach to developing these skills: some establish a formal modular development programme while others rely on more ad hoc methods. In our experience, if scale allows, a business's investment in creating a structured development programme provides demonstrable returns in terms of setting a common standard, raising the bar and creating a recognizable cadre of individuals within the HR function who are there to fulfil a distinct role. As good practice would suggest, a programme that combines an assessment and development planning component as well as the potential for integrating project-based action learning can also be very beneficial.

BUSINESS CONSULTING SKILLS

The Business Partner's need for formal skills development in all of the areas referred to in Figure 14.2 will depend on their previous experience. Those with a more traditional HR background may require more emphasis in strategy and business planning or project management, whilst individuals who may have come from a general business role may require more emphasis in change management or communication. A typical set of HR BP development modules are shown in Table 14.1, overleaf.

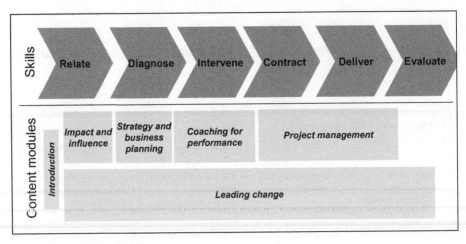

Source: Orion Partners (2005)

Figure 14.2 Suggested modules for Business Partner development

Table 14.1 Typical content models for the suggested modules for Business Partner development

Content modules	Topics covered
Introduction to Business Partnering	• Role of the HR BP • Aligning HR strategy • Skills for success • Measuring success
Impact and influence	• Levers of impact and influence • Personal styles and corporate cultures • Matching tactics to targets • Role plays and feedback • Improving influence
Strategy and business planning	• Review of company planning processes • Overview of strategic plans and imperatives • Overview of strategic planning tools • Identifying opportunities to lead
Coaching for performance	• Challenging your client's thinking • Listening/questioning • Knowing your audience • Effective presentation skills
Project management	• Scoping, planning and resourcing • Stakeholder management • Managing teams and budgets • Risk management • Strategies for when things go wrong
Leading change	• Understanding cycles of change • A model for change • Impact analysis • Journey management • Communicating for success

It should be possible for training in technical HR skills to be provided easily either through more traditional in-house development or via the wide range of professional development support available on the open market. The Business Partner must avoid slipping into the comfort zone of being the technical expert, but instead identify the most appropriate business application of any given HR intervention. In future, however, the challenge may be slightly different. As new HR models allow for a different approach to career management within the function, with the potential for more entrants from the line, fewer people will take the generalist route into HR that allowed a gradual acquisition of the core technical skill set. This development will be examined in more detail in Chapter 15.

KNOWLEDGE ACQUISITION

In Chapter 13 we made reference to the importance of context. The generic skills in the Business Partner's toolkit will be valid in any environment but the success of their application will depend significantly on the individual's knowledge and under-standing of the business in which they are operating. Figure 14.3 provides a typical overview of the knowledge components that a Business Partner should possess. There are four key areas:

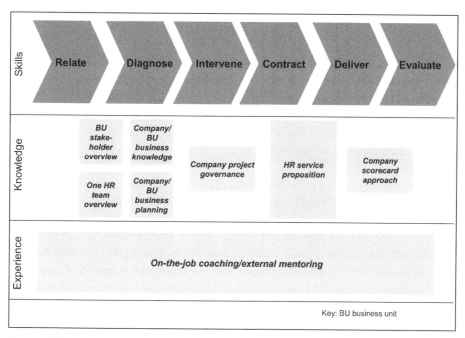

Source: Orion Partners (2005)

Figure 14.3 Typical knowledge and experience requirements for Business Partner development

- Knowledge of the company and business unit – why are we here and what's our future strategy?

- Detail of the HR proposition – how is HR organized to deliver?

- Company planning and project management – how do we plan and implement change?

- Company measurement approaches – how are we evaluated?

Acquisition of this knowledge can be left to chance and to a certain extent any Business Partner worth their salt will have the drive and tenacity to seek out the pertinent information of their own accord. However, in our experience, individuals will be more successful if more structured methods of knowledge sharing are made available – including standard documentation that is easily accessible, user friendly and up to date! Effective use of company intranets and formal knowledge-sharing events improve the efficiency and effectiveness of knowledge acquisition and help to build a sense of community within the HR function.

LEARNING FROM EXPERIENCE

Formal development is obviously important, but nothing beats experience. This should be the mantra for all HR BPs. At every level organizations respect advisers and leaders who have the 'scars to prove it'. This will be particularly true for HR as it seeks to engage the business in delivering change or strategic direction, because organizations have traditionally not seen that from HR. It is also invaluable when shaping the agenda for each role in the model. Experience of what the organization needs and what will work is a vital touch-point when other skills are being applied to achieve the goal; it prevents the incumbent from developing solutions that will be ineffective in that particular environment.

If training programmes in the classroom or on-line are relied upon, the breadth of learning required can never be achieved. Mentoring programmes, for example, provide the individual with a new viewpoint on the challenges facing HR as well as exposure to key decision-makers in the organization. Furthermore, opinion formers who provide this support get a sense of how HR is developing and building its capability to deliver in its new role. Exposure to secondments internally and externally can build skills that may not be found in an HR function that is in transition to the HR BP model. Bringing these together can create very powerful contextualized development programmes that not only support the growth of HR's capability, but support the change programme as well.

KEY THEMES IN ROLE DEVELOPMENT ACTIVITIES

- *Transition from operational to strategic roles:* Clearly one of the key objectives of introducing the Business Partner role is to promote HR's shift from a reactive to a proactive, strategically driven function. Much of this work happens in the Strategic Partner role described by Ulrich.[1] It also needs to be evident in the more senior levels of the other roles. This shift is one of the hardest to manage in general managers, let alone in HR professionals. It requires a deep understanding of the business's operating environment, strategic direction and execution evaluation metrics. The ability to appraise, plan and execute change in this way is not learned through a single development intervention. It requires the reflection and experience that only exposure to managers, thinkers and activities outside HR can bring. As the most high-profile and 'glamorous' side of the work, the Strategic Partner role will also be where most people will gravitate to. Few will be able to deliver, and selection will become important in assessing who will benefit most from this development in the first place.

- *Laying the foundations:* Technical HR knowledge provides the function with credibility, and key skills like basic relationship management can be learned simply in managing a range of suppliers in a Shared Service function. The Business Partner model shows that both types of skill, technical and generic, must be established if the right solutions are to be implemented at a technical level. As the development planning is completed for all roles, opportunities to develop these skills must be found. Without them future HR BPs will never have the technical skills to support their analysis and execution.

- *Business education:* HR has typically followed a well-trodden path in business education terms: chartered status, followed by an MA in Human Resource Management for senior staff. The quality of the business school's reputation may not have been a key issue in selecting these courses. In addition, the credibility in the business that a management qualification provides an HR executive has been rarely considered. In the HR BP model the qualification a person has must be more focused on the demands of the role. Technical HR skills can be developed along the way. A qualification that provides a 'key' to the minds of business leaders and operational experts is of far more value here. It will build credibility far faster, and provide a framework within which the HR BP can hang other experience. As such the MBA route, in the case of Strategic Partners, will be of greater value than the

---

1   Ulrich, D. (1997) *Human Resource Champions: The Next Agenda for Adding Value and Delivery Results,* Harvard Business School Press.

MA in Human Resource Management. The MSc in Operational Management will be more useful for the Administrative Expert in HR. The financial and strategic analysis skills, coupled with the language of colleagues in marketing and procurement, will provide an unrivalled context for further development of HR staff.

- *Holistic development planning:* requires the incumbent to develop skills within the context of the role's operating environment. This means using all the development tools available to HR.

CHAPTER 15

Selection and Career Management for Business Partners

SELECTION OF HR BPs

The aim of this chapter is not to describe in detail the recruitment and selection process, which will vary in practice from organization to organization, but to consider some of the issues around the selection of HR Business Partners and propose some approaches.

'It is a truth universally acknowledged, that …' selecting the right employees is one of the most critical of all managerial responsibilities. It is essential therefore that thought and time are invested in the process and that the recruitment strategy is aligned to the goals of the business. This is particularly true of the HR BP role – the role is often part of a new HR approach in the organization and so must be defined carefully to ensure that selectors understand how to find candidates and what they are looking for, and that clarity is provided to candidates.

THE CHANGING FACE OF HR RECRUITMENT

A quick scan of the HR trade press will show how different the vacancy adverts for the HR BP role are from the traditional HR manager role. Taking this assessment further some key differences emerge in a number of areas. Looking at the Group HR Business Partner adverts in Figure 15.1, a number of themes emerge.

SELECTION CRITERIA

- *Qualifications:* One difference between the jobs advertised in Figure 15.1 from the traditional HR management role is immediately apparent – no professional qualification is required. The requirements of the role have moved far beyond the narrow confines of the qualification at any level. Specialism in HR practice can be useful, but without the qualifications to engage the business they are of little use to the HR Business Partner. As a result the recruitment criteria need to become more expansive than they have traditionally been in HR.

Group HR Business Partner

'We'll look to you to develop and implement policies that encompass everything from pay and benefits ... to the effective use of SAP.'

'Whilst an advantage, a **CIPD qualification is not essential**. Far more important is your experience of thinking for the longer term and translating strategies into policies and practices.'

'So expect to draw on your ... talent for diplomacy as you travel to sites across the country, **building relationships with key stakeholders**.'

European HR Business Partner

'You will **liaise with the HR Shared Services Group** to identify, package ... and deliver employee development programmes.'

'Other areas of activity include coordinating the annual pay determination process ... **and managing the local Centre of Excellence process**.'

Senior HR Business Partner Partner, Contact Centres

'Operational HR issues will be dealt with on a day-to-day basis by the HR Shared Service Centre, making this a largely strategic role.'

'You will be able to **demonstrate a strong understanding of operational issues and technology** ... This will have allowed you to **implement business improvement programmes that capture the synergy between people and IT** in the contact centre environment.'

Figure 15.1   A selection of recruitment adverts

- *Virtual team management:* The roles advertised in Figure 15.1 all look for Business Partners to 'liaise' with other parts of the HR delivery team, including line managers, HR Shared Services and HR Centres of Excellence. The need for engagement and remote management skills must be made explicit in the recruitment criteria. The HR BP will have little in the way of direct resources to throw at a problem but still be expected to deliver; thus the ability to use intelligently all the assets available is central to the role and should be used as a key criterion to sift candidates.

- *Explicit role focus:* The outcomes expected are clearly articulated in the adverts in Figure 15.1. The focus is not on inputs to the job role, for example technical knowledge, but on the ability to apply these and deliver tangible outcomes for the recruiting organization. The adverts in Figure 15.1 indicate clearly that they do not expect the incumbent to tie themselves up with activities that other parts of HR are already delivering. Staying in the comfort zone of HR administrative processes is not acceptable.

- *Experience:* The adverts in Figure 15.1 do not specify 'X-years' experience' in HR. They focus instead on business experience which will allow the incumbent to deliver solutions that are credible with line managers and really target the organization's issues. These roles rely on the right applicants having the relevant operational experience and understanding tied to the knowledge of how to leverage the tools at HR's disposal. Without experience of how the business units they are serving deploy their people, processes and technology, the HR BP will fail to assess the issues accurately and be unable to craft the appropriate solutions.

RECRUITMENT CHANNELS

The HR BP role also requires a reappraisal of the recruitment channels that are used if recruitment is to be effective and credible within the marketplace.

- *The media:* Is *People Management*, as a key UK HR publication, still going to deliver when the role occupant may not be or have ever been a member of the Chartered Institute of Personnel Development? As a role that places business analysis at its heart, recruitment advertisements in the quality broadsheet sector are being used more and more and potential applicants will be looking and thinking more widely than the HR press, so it makes sense to target these.

- *Search:* When faced with an immature market for HR BPs that has few candidates of deep quality and experience, a focused search firm will offer a far more efficient solution than advertising. The search firm can also advise on the sort of remuneration package required to secure a candidate, as this may be very different to that used by (or earned) by the current HR function. However, it should not be assumed that the search firm automatically understands the role you are looking for since it is as new to search firms as it is to HR teams.

- *Internal recruitment:* This channel brings significant risks and rewards. On the risk side the selection of the individuals from the internal pool may leave the organization with 'old wine in new bottles'. Since the internal HR function may have rarely been involved in the kind of activities that HR BPs engage in, it is unlikely that all the talent can be found in the in-house HR team. However, the internal marketplace can yield two useful sources of candidates. People management is a key skill of any good manager and as such the HR BP role can be a great means to expose high fliers within the company to the kind of strategic analysis work, high-volume process management or complex change project/programme work that lies at the heart of the HR BP model. Recruiting internally can also be a means to 'refresh the function's DNA'. Candidates from the operational or financial side of the business will bring in a perspective to people management that will challenge and promote a business-led focus for the role. Hiring from within also signals to the business that HR is serious about delivering the organization's objectives and providing a business-focused service.

- *Network:* Good HR Business Partners use their network, and so their network should be a good means of recruiting them. At the most senior levels those presenting at conferences and professional forums form the most obvious targets. Certain companies in the UK and US are also now gathering a reputation for successful implementation of the model at these events. This provides an indication of the pedigree of the talent they are fostering which other companies should notice when their former employees come onto the market. Whilst these networks may not be the most efficient and transparent sources of candidates, they may provide access to a 'star' performance that can set the benchmark for candidates from internal or external sources who are recruited in a more conventional way.

Example of an HR BP assessment centre approach

The following approach is based on a model used for a recent client of Orion Partners to select senior HR BPs to roles in the c£60k+ salary range.

First round
9 am–9.30 am: Welcome by Business Unit HR Director – sets the context for the event

9.30 am–11 am: Group business analysis exercise – assesses candidates' business/financial analysis skills and interpersonal skills

11 am–12.30 pm: Individual HR planning and strategy execution exercise – aims to assess the candidates' understanding of linkages between strategy and execution. It also examines their ability to identify the key drivers and means by which to execute an HR strategy

1.30 pm–3 pm: Interview with Business Unit HR Director and senior non-HR business managers – allows the customer (the business) to shape selection and test experience and cultural fit

Second round

Interview with Group HR Director and Business Unit HR Director

Interview with Business Unit Managing Director

This model represents a considerable investment in selection centre set-up and management time. This was felt to be critical in ensuring that the business bought into the successful candidate once they had been selected, and that the successful candidate had the right skills, knowledge and behaviours to deliver.

It is worth noting that testing financial and numerical reasoning may also be a relevant tool for more junior roles, although it was not considered necessary at this level.

SOME OF THE CHALLENGES

Through the research conducted for this chapter and the book in general, the following challenges stand out as those that need to be addressed during the development of any career management framework for Business Partners.

- These HR BP roles are highly visible and they need the appropriate support.

- Can the current incumbents change? A rule of thumb, based on recent experience, suggests that 20 per cent can and do naturally, 30 per cent can with the right development support but as many as 50 per cent either cannot or will not. Being honest about this as a reality is probably a good starting point.

- Be honest about whether people can make the transition through the career paths and selection process.

- Don't underestimate the need to train people for the new roles.

The career management approach for all the Business Partner roles must address these. To fail to do so, will undermine the success of any implementation.

CAREER MANAGEMENT FOR BUSINESS PARTNERS

In 2003 the Chartered Institute of Personnel and Development published a survey, *Managing Employee Careers*, which concluded that: 'The career landscape has clearly moved from a paternalistic approach where employers guide employees through a career path within an organisation, to employees now being expected to take responsibility for their own career development'. Changes in the size and shape of organizations, delayering and reduced hierarchies, have meant that there are fewer opportunities for the employee to develop their career in a single organization and still less a single department. Lateral (intra- and inter-company) career moves are expected if the employee is to develop breadth of experience; work–life balance has become more of an issue for people and short-term, interim or project work is now more common. Individuals are explicitly expected to take far more responsibility for their own career management. It is against this background that organizations must position the career management of their HR Business Partners. There is no 'one size fits all' best practice that is appropriate in today's environment, so what is described below are pointers that will help organizations and individuals to find an optimal approach.

We have argued above that the numbers of 'traditional career' opportunities are disappearing. Nowadays the use of the word 'career' covers a wide range of occupational experiences, not just a succession of jobs with increasing pay and responsibility. A 'career' does not necessarily involve promotion or progression, and may increasingly mean moves across occupational and organizational boundaries. One trap that organizations should be very careful not to fall into is the creation of multiple layers of Business Partner just to provide development opportunities. This may be tempting when the organization is transitioning from a more traditional structure, as the leap from an HR manager to Business Partner may be quite a large one. However, it creates a high risk of diluting and undermining the real impact of the Business Partner role. We would advise a maximum of two layers, where a more senior Business Partner may take responsibility for managing other Business Partners. We have seen up to five levels – not the best example of streamlined organization design!

If a career is a sequence of jobs that are not necessarily connected by industrial or professional experience, career management must be a dynamic process, continually adjusted in the light of changing organizational circumstances. HR is probably more guilty than most of being the 'cobbler's child' (always the least well shod) regarding their careers. The traditional HR career path is disappearing, which means a different approach is required to HR 'career planning'. If the competencies and skills discussed above are required, then how can these be developed through career management?

Figure 15.2 takes some of the skills and example competencies we discussed in Chapter 13 and examines how they can be developed. It shows how these might best be developed through an individual taking on a series of business, project and functional jobs that form a significantly more varied path than is traditional in those working in the HR function. The starting point is the most immediately striking feature: the individual's career is launched from a non-HR background. Working as an operations manager builds the employee's key business management skills and immerses them in the 'nuts and bolts' of the business.

The aspiring HR Business Partner then formally moves into the HR function. Here they build their technical knowledge and are exposed to a diverse range of managers. Operating in a Business Partner role, within a limited team, with few (if any) direct reports, the individual is required to develop the skills and competencies around coaching and consulting that allow them to achieve results through virtual teams (teams that are not physically located together or part of the same business unit).

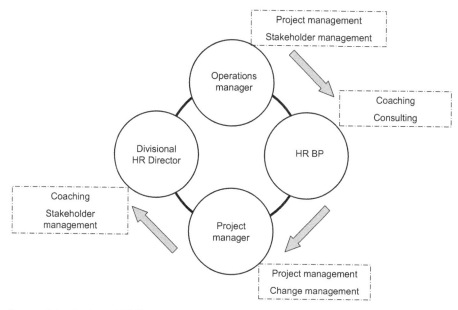

Source: Orion Partners (2005)

Figure 15.2   Typical HR career path

The individual's next move could be into a project management role where their ability to deliver change will be honed. Project management roles tend to focus on aggressively delivering real step changes in business performance while line roles tend to focus on incremental change. As a result, project management roles can be very powerful in equipping the Business Partner with the experience and capability to see those project opportunities more readily in line management roles. They also provide for a solid foundation in stakeholder management.

The individual's next move is to take up a leadership role to fully develop their strategic instinct and capabilities. The exposure to general management issues, either in an HR role (as in Figure 15.2) or as a more typical general manager, provides the individual with the strategic formulation and, more importantly, delivery skills and competencies required.

It is worth reviewing the link to Ulrich's model.[1] In Figure 15.3 the alignment of each element of our individual's career with Ulrich's holistic overview of HR can be seen. This provides useful validation that HR does not happen only in HR: an HR professional can develop outside HR and can be highly or, as is argued here, more

---

1   Ulrich, D. (1997) *Human Resource Champions: The Next Agenda for Adding Value and Delivery Results,* Harvard Business School Press

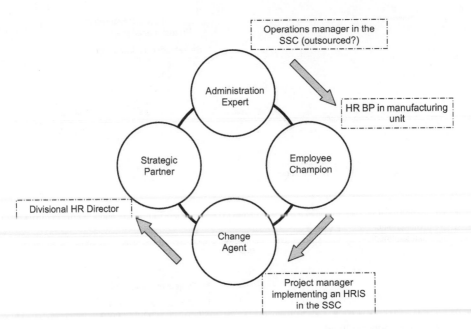

Figure 15.3   Example of a career management model aligned with the Ulrich
model

effective by passing through other functional areas. Indeed, this has been identified as
a key component of a successful delivery model for HR and one that should be rolled
out across the business in other functional areas.

The typical career path illustrated in Figure 15.3 becomes particularly powerful if
the development opportunities are selected to address the issues the business faces.
For example:

- *Non-HR permanent roles:* Stakeholder management and operational
  understanding and credibility can be developed if HR staff are selected from
  or spend time in jobs outside the HR function. Experience at the heart of the
  business gives HR professionals access to an intuitive understanding of the
  business's requirements when shaping the HR agenda.

- *Sideways job changes:* Staff moving from other parts of the business into HR
  for a period can be a way of infusing the HR team with business experience
  and developing in them the technical skills needed in HR, both of which are
  thus built within the context of current business issues. Arguably these
  members of staff are also being absorbed and assimilated with a healthy dose
  of realism about what the 'ivory tower' of an HR-centric view of the business
  can achieve.

- *Secondment:* Giving HR professionals experience in project management in business-led projects rather than HR-led projects can be driven through internal secondment. These opportunities have the additional benefit of building HR's presence and credibility within other parts of the business, as well as building the key skills of change delivery in the HR staff. Some organizations will also take this concept further and consider secondments to clients or suppliers.

- *Leadership exposure:* Providing the HR BP with exposure to general management issues within divisional leadership roles cements their understanding of strategic and financial issues, before they take on the most senior HR BP roles. Figure 15.3 shows the individual assuming an HR divisional director role, but arguably, dependent upon the business and HR's requirements, other general management positions may be appropriate.

Whatever the approach, the nature of the continuum, the accumulation of skills, is the most important factor in play here. Building a coherent route for developing the HR BP that is aligned with the business environment and objectives offers the most effective approach to developing in them the skills and competencies required, and the greatest business benefit. As is explored in the sections of this chapter that follow the starting point of recruitment and the formal and informal development approaches used can offer a powerful support to this kind of career pathing in HR.

WHAT IS HAPPENING ON THE GROUND TODAY?

It is interesting to note that the starting point for the HR BP career path is being found more and more outside HR. We recently assisted a client in transferring senior operational managers into key senior Business Partner roles, which provided vital business credibility to the new model and reassured the business that the HR BP model could deliver a step change in HR performance.[2]

It should be noted that transferring staff is not a panacea. It is still the case that the majority of senior HR staff are not 'parachuted' in from roles and careers that have been external to HR and research suggests that successful HR functions which deliver strategically are not dominated by external hires.[3] Taking the career management approach of moving between functions, the individual must look for a balance that addresses how the business perceives HR and the objectives the HR Business Partners will have. The issue is one of credibility to gain the access to deliver. In businesses

---

2   Orion Partners (2004) *Research on Major Public Sector HR BP Implementation.*
3   Kelly, J. and Gennard, J. (2001) *Power and Influence in the Boardroom: The Role of the Personnel/HR Director*, Routledge, p. 70.

where HR has a strong and well-respected voice, it may not matter that HR executives begin their careers externally to HR, providing HR has the right business acumen and vocabulary. Nonetheless, a recent survey of CEOs found that 35 per cent of CEOs looked for non-HR/line management experience in their senior HR Directors because, they said, they wanted people with credibility and the ability to align HR to organizational objectives – the very reasons we have discussed.[4]

It appears that, as the role of the HR Business Partner develops, experience external to HR is becoming an essential requirement to their career. Looking back to the shift in emphasis away from technical HR skills to non-traditional HR skills, it is useful to ask what range of experience in HR is actually essential. Recent research suggests that a broad range of HR experience is as important as the external experience.[5] Where HR is operating as a full Strategic Partner, 44 per cent of senior HR staff had a broad range of experience across 'generalist HR'. The authors of this research argue that the reason for the success of these staff is their wide range of experience in HR technical subjects aligned with business understanding gained from other roles than that of the Business Partner. This application of HR technical knowledge to business issues is seen as being the key factor. The support mechanisms discussed in Chapters 3 and 4 (Shared Services or Centres of Excellence) provide the deep technical knowledge the HR BP needs.

Ultimately the balance between HR and non-HR experience is what is key. As the HR BP moves through the range of roles identified earlier in this chapter, they are developing the competencies that will provide HR with a new ability to deliver. Without for example the project management experience the HR BP has gained from delivering a technology project, the skills for delivering business change will not be available to HR and practised there. HR technical skills alone can never provide this richness and will leave the HR BP ill equipped to deliver.

THE ROLE OF SUCCESSION MANAGEMENT

One key feature of career management is that of succession management. The Business Partner is still a relatively rare beast in the marketplace at any level. As has been discussed, the skills, knowledge and behaviours of the HR BP are not found in the usual HR team member's portfolio as a complete package. This means that picking candidates out from the open recruitment market with the lure of a higher reward package may not yield results. At the moment the Business Partner model is still

---

4 Kelly, J. and Gennard, J. (2001) *Power and Influence in the Boardroom: The Role of the Personnel/HR Director*, Routledge, p. 77.
5 Lawler, Edward and Mohrman, Susan (2003) 'HR as a Strategic Partner: What Does it Take to Make it Happen?', *Human Resource Planning*, pp. 23–4.

limited in its take up. Where it has been implemented, HR BPs are in the early stages of their learning curve, so the opportunities to 'poach' talent are restricted. This clearly points to the need to deploy robust succession-planning models.

The holistic nature of the HR model proposed by the likes of Ulrich presents an interesting challenge to those who seek to 'grow their own'. As members of staff move through the career pathways reviewed above, some may choose not to move on to develop the full range of skills needed for the HR BP. Their career aspirations may be met by the attractions of process management, acting as an Administrative Expert or managing part of an HR Shared Service Centre (SSC). Indeed, many HR staff have begun to carve out separate career paths solely in this area, from managing teams in the SSC to running the centres on a single-country or global scale. The area has grown to such an extent that complex, challenging roles are now widely available in that area.

As a result, those managing careers and succession planning for HR need to be mindful of the fact that some potential HR BPs will be lost along the way. As with any succession-planning exercise, the usual rewards and motivational tools must be used to keep the developing HR BPs in the organization – particularly as they are becoming a more valuable commodity on the open recruitment market.

CHAPTER 16

Lessons Learnt Implementing the HR BP Model

IMPLEMENTATION LESSONS LEARNT

Orion Partners have been involved in the implementation of upward of 14 different HR Business Partner initiatives in the public and private sectors. We have not always got it right first time nor have we always accurately assessed the size of the mouthful relative to our ability to chew. This final chapter deals with the lessons that we have learnt at the implementation coal-face, where the theory meets reality. We have identified 12 key common issues that need to be addressed in a successful implementation.

1. Get the basics right first – This may seem obvious but unless the basic HR provision is of the right standard there will be very limited business appetite for discussions about strategy. Business Partnering will only be a credible concept when the bread and butter HR service delivery works well. Launching business partnering without the solid foundation of reliable transactional service delivery will only damage credibility. For example, if your cannot pay people accurately on time, month in month out, then fix that first before you attempt to offer strategic advice.

2. Get clarity on the role – often HRBPs know what they're not supposed to be doing – for example, the routine transactional HR activity, but there is limited definition as to what they should be doing. This often leads to a dilution of the role as people fall back into their comfort zone by proving an HR generalist service. Organizations need to be able to clearly describe the types of business outcomes they expect their business partners to focus on and deliver. Orion Partners have found a good starting point can be to paint the picture through describing in detail a typical 'Year in the Life of an HRBP'. This can be really helpful in illustrating the difference between the traditional generalist and the BP role. An example is shown at the end of this chapter.

3. 'Educate' and involve the line – often it's the business managers that are not ready for the introduction of the HRBP role. If they have not experienced the sort of value that a strategic approach to HR can deliver then they will not know what to expect and will probably not know how to

engage with the HRBP most usefully. In our experience, creating the three or four clear business-related deliverables for the HRBP to focus on in the first six months after launch will give the BP the right opportunities to demonstrate how they can make a real difference. The business will generally come looking for more of the same if they can see early tangible business results.

4. Don't overlayer – There can be a tendency to build in hierarchies into the BP structure which reflect the more traditional HR career paths. This often leads to mini HR departments being built up under BPs rather than the BP making more effective use of the benefits of the shared service and policy centres of excellence. At most there should be two levels of business partner. We have found that giving an HRBP neither budget nor resource is an effective way to ensure they the leverage the other elements of the service model (for example, shared services) most effectively. By taking away a dedicated budget the HRBP must sell their projects to either the HR Director or to their business leaders in order to secure specific funding. This is an excellent way to ensure that what gets done matters to the business rather than mattering to the HR function.

5. Recognize the new skills requirements and offer relevant support – The skills requirements of an effective Business Partner are quite distinct from those of a traditional HR generalist. While HR technical skills provide a useful grounding for the role, they are not what make for long-term success. The priority skills areas are in impact and influence, relationship management, problem solving and analysis. It goes without saying that this needs to be accompanied by strong commercial acumen and a real understanding of the business that the HRBP is operating in. Recognizing these requirements when implementing the model is key. This will often mean a robust assessment and selection process and a development programme that helps individuals address any skills gaps. We have typically found that an HRBP will require between four to eight days of retraining to support the move away from a generalist background.

6. Change the work as well as the job title – Many HRBP implementations can be nothing more than a rebadging exercise – same output but a different job title. However, the appearance of the HRBP label can raise expectations amongst business leaders for a more strategic HR service and if what they get is more of the same (and often at increased cost) then disillusionment and disengagement soon results. You need to keep your business partners away from managing the transactional work – many HRBPs have built up a credible career out of managing the administration

and are very happy to continue to do so, if given the opportunity, rather than working with the business to deliver value. This can be more damaging than sticking with a traditional HR approach. It will also de-motivate those in HR who can see how the role should work and who become frustrated by the new organization and by their less effective colleagues. The hand-offs and role boundaries between the shared service, HRBPs and the Centre of Excellence (CofE) need to be defined and adhered to.

7. Parade your successes and market your new model – Make sure you track and capture improvements in service and positive feedback from HR's customers. Ensure that monthly reports present a balanced story of successes and achievements. Trumpet your successes but also accurately report service issues and publish associated improvement action plans to show that you have a grasp of the delivery challenges and are taking steps to resolve them. When the business starts to see tangible evidence of the linkages between effective people management and improvements in business performance, HR becomes genuinely involved in business planning and will be held accountable for delivering their part of the business strategy. The business partner role will then truly personify the shift from admin. resource to valued service provider.

8. Build a 'one HR' mindset – the division of the function into shared services, business partners and centres of excellence can reduce the feel of belonging to one professional community. It is easy for each element of the new HR organization to begin to blame the others for any service failures. Relationships, especially if there are significant geographic distance between work locations, may weaken and contacts loosen. The HR leadership team should ensure that the function is given the opportunity to meet face to face at 'town hall' style meetings. Senior leaders from the HRSS, CofEs, and the HRBPs should meet together to review progress, plan for the future and agree performance improvement priorities at least once a quarter. The use of functional newsletters (hard copy or on-line), web-discussion boards and a structured HR function engagement plan (allowing the two-way dissemination of profession-wide information) are important engagement tools for the HR Director to use to maintain the professional bonds across the new organization structure.

9. Reconnect the career paths – the realignment of the function can result in the traditional routes to skill development and career progression being broken. Orion have worked with many firms to create credible career paths that allow progress through the shared service centre into HRBP roles and then on to senior director-level positions. By building in specific

development posts, managing succession planning and engaging in skill development at the individual level it is possible to sell the new roles in HR as attractive stepping stones for the ambitious professional.

10. Regularly review your service offerings – The needs of the business will change and the HRBP as a important role to play in articulating the change of requirements to the other parts of the HR service model. The account and service managers in the shared service centres need to talk with the HRBP at least annually to collect their views and predictions for the changing requirements of the business. Holding an open and honest discussion about what is working well and what would could be made even better is a vital dialogue

11. Prepare to make some tough calls post-implementation – The HR Director will probably need to move or replace a small number of under-performing HRBPs within the first 12 months of launching a programme. The strategic and personal influencing skills required of the role are often beyond the capability of many competent HR generalists. If those who have shown themselves not to be up to the task are not dealt with then their lack of delivery will undermine the credibility of the HR transformation programme.

12. Involve the HRBP in service development and process improvement planning – the HRBP is probably closer to their business than any other member of the HR team. They need to have a voice in the prioritization of service improvement in the shared service centre. They should also assist in advising on any proposed changes in policy and procedure which will impact their business. These inputs should be structured and regular – Orion recommend quarterly reviews with representatives of the whole HR function to review the overall look and feel of the HR service and to agree where the function will devote its energies to better meeting customer expectations.

A YEAR IN THE LIFE OF AN HR BUSINESS PARTNER

The following table illustrates a year in the life of a typical HRBP from a variety of perspectives: planning, performance management, reward, learning and development, acquisition, employee relations and organizational design.

Table 16.1   A year in the life of an HR Business Partner – Illustrative

	Business Planning	Resourcing Planning	Business Performance/ Performance Management	Reward	Learning and Development	Acquisitions	Employee/ Industrial Relations	Org. Design
January	Inform business budgeting process based on future resource needs/possible organizational change, and so on Develop HRBP budget for new financial year working with HR Director and Finance	Determine resourcing strategy for next financial year based on budget/ resourcing needs/ trends in employment market	Develop presentations to support company-wide performance management presentations Cascade presentations ensuring managers can present to all members in their team					
February	Sign off HRBP budget					Work with business to determine possible approach to targeted acquisitions		Lead a review of the OD of the marketing function

Continued

	Business Planning	Resourcing Planning	Business Performance/ Performance Management	Reward	Learning and Development	Acquisitions	Employee/ Industrial Relations	Org. Design
March						Develop communications strategy to support possible future acquisitions Engage external legal advice to support on acquisition process – in relation to employment law in overseas organization	Commence consultation with trades unions on review of marketing function	Continue with marketing review
April	Partake in six-monthly business performance review Review impact of HR strategy on business performance/ making recommendations as appropriate	Assist Business Director in reshaping key first report role after current incumbent leaves			In conjunction with L&D specialists review output of development plans	Undertake due diligence for possible acquisition		Develop proposal for a new marketing function which includes outsourcing some services and operating with a reduced headcount

Continued

	Business Planning	Resourcing Planning	Business Performance/ Performance Management	Reward	Learning and Development	Acquisitions	Employee/ Industrial Relations	Org. Design
	Key recommendations are associated with sales force effectiveness							Present proposal to business leadership team
May		Act as an assessor in the recruitment of new member of leadership team	Lead workstream to review sales performance and effectiveness of sales force		Develop key L&D initiatives for next 12 months based on above review Work with L&D specialists to present proposed initiatives to business leadership team	Develop and present plans for possible acquisition to include Retention strategy How to address differences in culture Working with the trades unions in the target company Harmonization of terms and conditions of employment Integration of new organization	Further consultation with trades unions on marketing department proposal	

Continued

	Business Planning	Resourcing Planning	Business Performance/ Performance Management	Reward	Learning and Development	Acquisitions	Employee/ Industrial Relations	Org. Design
June		Negotiate package for successful candidate. Oversee job offer	Develop approach to determining what makes a 'successful sales person' including development of sales specific competencies. Present approach to leadership	Aligned to the successful sales person project and working with in-house reward specialists develop a diagnostic tool to measure the effectiveness of current sales reward scheme	Review L&D priorities based on six-monthly business performance review giving emphasis to sales performance and selling skills		Develop material for trades unions consultation re. sales force effectiveness and sales force reward – present at trades union consultation meeting	Communicate proposed changes to marketing department to employees
July				Undertake focus groups with sales teams re. reward		Undertake further due diligence on target acquisition. Develop transition plan and communications plan for target acquisition		
August			Programme manage the development of	Commission in house reward team to develop		Support business director with the negotiation of		Provide input to strategy for finding an

Continued

	Business Planning	Resourcing Planning	Business Performance/ Performance Management	Reward	Learning and Development	Acquisitions	Employee/ Industrial Relations	Org. Design
			sales competencies	new sales reward scheme	deals for target senior executives subject to acquisition going ahead			outsource partner for marketing department
September			Programme manage the development of sales competencies			Acquisition completed	Present an update on sales force effectiveness and sales force reward at the trades unions consultation meeting Present acquisition update to trades unions Continue with consultation re. marketing department	Provide input to requests for information for marketing department outsource
October			Develop new self-assessment tools	Review proposed sales reward		Implement communications		

Continued

	Business Planning	Resourcing Planning	Business Performance/ Performance Management	Reward	Learning and Development	Acquisitions	Employee/ Industrial Relations	Org. Design
			for sales employees	changes with in-house reward team		and transition plans for acquired company		
November	Work with executive team on next 18 months' strategy/includes consideration of possible additional acquisitions		Present competencies and self-assessment tools to business leadership team	Present new sales reward scheme to leadership team – aligned to competencies and self-assessment tools			Present an update on sales force effectiveness and sales force reward at the trades unions consultation meeting Continue consultation re. marketing department	Play a lead role in reviewing marketing and department bids against agreed criteria
December		Work with resourcing team to ascertain trends in recruitment ahead of next years budgeting and planning cycle	Incorporate new competencies and self-assessment tools into the performance management process – to be launched at next years performance review	Develop communications including the production of a CD-ROM supporting the new sales reward scheme.				

Index

About the Authors

Ian Hunter is a founding partner of Orion Partners. He worked for a number of leading management consultancies, including Accenture and AT Kearney, focusing on the areas of HR transformation, outsourcing, Shared Services and Business Partnering. Educated at Bristol and Warwick Universities and London Business School he has held executive HR management roles with organizations such as British Petroleum and PepsiCo.

Jane Saunders is one of the founding partners of Orion Partners. Jane is an experienced international consultant, with significant experience in the area of HR strategy and transformation. She combines a practical expertise of operational HR delivery, with the consulting experience of shaping and delivering innovative and effective HR solutions. After a degree in Modern Languages at Oxford, Jane embarked on a career in HR that has taken her from food manufacturing, through property to professional services. Prior to joining Orion, she held senior roles in both Accenture's HR outsourcing division and its change management consultancy. She has worked in all areas of HR transformation but in her recent consulting work has focused on service and organization design with a particular emphasis on bringing the commercial disciplines of service and account management to the HR function.

Simon Constance is a senior consultant at Orion Partners. Simon has hands-on business development, HR transformation consulting and operational management experience. On graduating from Liverpool University, Simon began a career in supply chain and operations management in the logistics and FMCG sectors. After moving into HR, he completed an MA in Human Resource Management at Newcastle University, and then joined Accenture where he focused on HR transformation, Shared Services and outsourcing. His recent consulting work has seen him concentrate on the role of the HR Business Partner and the development of operational excellence in Shared Services through the design and implementation of financial control, change management and operations management approaches.

Allan Boroughs, a partner with Orion Partners, has an extensive track record in the design and delivery of HR information technology spanning a 15-year period. Initially trained as a work-study engineer, Allan applied his knowledge to the development of management information systems within HR and the streamlining of associated processes. Prior to Orion, Allan worked in business development for a niche consulting firm and as leader of Atos KPMG Consulting's HR information technology practice for

Financial Services. Allan has led a wide range of global systems delivery projects in blue chip organizations.

For Product Safety Concerns and Information please contact our EU
representative GPSR@taylorandfrancis.com Taylor & Francis Verlag GmbH,
Kaufingerstraße 24, 80331 München, Germany

Printed and bound by CPI Group (UK) Ltd, Croydon, CR0 4YY
01/05/2025
01858428-0002